MODELLING

BASED ON · CITY AND GUILDS SUGARCRAFT COURSE

ELAINE MACGREGOR

MEREHURST

I wish to thank my husband, Stuart, for all his help with the writing and for all the designs and line drawings; British Bakels for the sugarpaste used in this book; Eunice Borchers for first interesting me in figure modelling; Steve Benison for introducing me to Fox; and Tombi Peck for her encouragement and friendship.

≈

Published in 1994 by Merehurst Limited, Ferry House,
51–57 Lacy Road, Putney, London SW15 1PR

ISBN 1 85391 355 3

Managing Editor Bridget Jones
Edited by Alison Leach
Designed by Jo Tapper
Photography by Zul Mukhida
Colour separation by Fotographics Limited, UK-Hong Kong
Printed by Wing King Tong, Hong Kong

NOTES ON USING THE RECIPES
For all recipes, quantities are given in metric, Imperial and cup measurements. Follow one set of measures only as they are not interchangeable. Standard 5ml teaspoons (tsp) and 15ml tablespoons (tbsp) are used. Australian readers, whose tablespoons measure 20ml, should adjust quantities accordingly. All spoon measures are assumed to be level unless otherwise stated.
Eggs are a standard size 3 (medium) unless otherwise stated.

CONTENTS

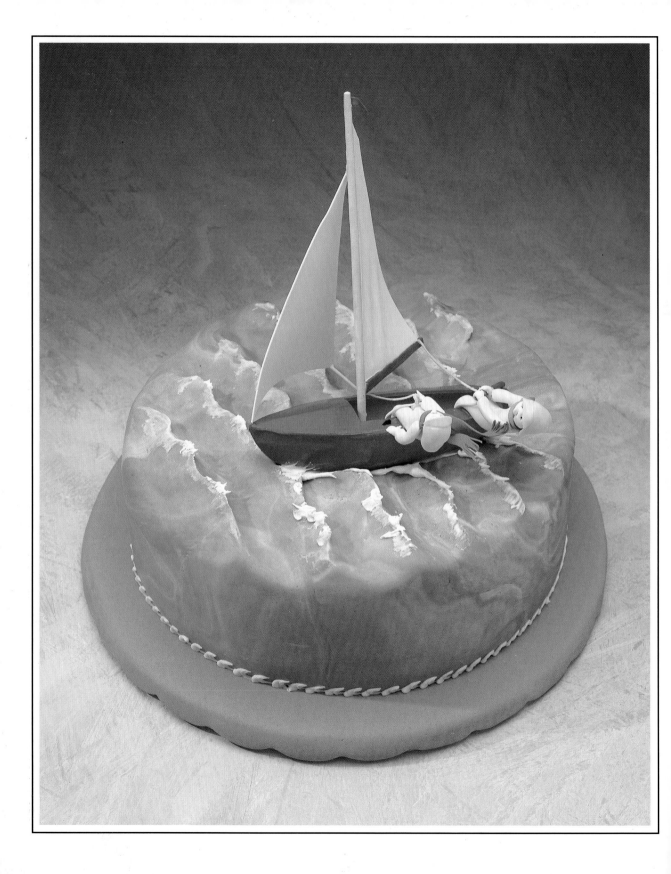

INTRODUCTION

Most of the time I bake cakes and decorate them for my clients – usually wedding and anniversary cakes – so I have little time to experiment. Writing this book has provided an opportunity for me to develop some of the ideas I have had for using sugarpaste and pastillage, and to confirm my feeling that they are two of the most versatile of modelling materials.

Pastillage, which is essentially sugar mixed with edible gums or gelatine to make it into a paste, has many forms. Some are very elastic, some extremely smooth and some dry quickly and become very hard. It is important to understand the differences and use the right kind for each job. For 'structural' models like walls, furniture and most large objects, a hard-drying paste is needed, whereas for drapes, curtains and clothing, a more elastic, slow-drying material is ideal. Flowers and braided or delicate items such as rope or hair, require something in between. In the designs, where different varieties are needed, I have indicated the type of mixture that I find works best for me.

When you are modelling, do take advice from others, especially if you admire their work, but be very cautious about the instant expert who claims to know the precise and only correct solution to every difficulty you may encounter! The more I have learned about sugarcraft, the more convinced I have become that there are many different ways of achieving a particular objective.

There are times when the pastillage just will not work the way I want it to, and on these occasions I accept the limitations of the medium and re-arrange my design accordingly. I console myself with the thought that like diplomacy, sugar modelling is the art of the possible, but unlike diplomacy it is not half as dangerous!

ROYAL ICING

❖

15g (½ oz/5 tsp) pure powdered albumen
90ml (3 fl oz/6 tbsp) water
500g (1 lb/3 cups) icing (confectioners') sugar,
sifted

Stir the albumen into the water and leave for 30 minutes until the coagulated mixture has dissolved. Strain into a mixing bowl and add half the sugar, then beat at the slowest speed if using an electric mixer, or for 100 strokes by hand, until smooth. Add the remaining sugar and continue beating for about 10 minutes at low speed. The icing is the right consistency when it has a satin-like appearance and stands in soft peaks.

Royal icing can also be made with natural egg white in the following proportions: 375g (12 oz/2¼ cups) icing sugar to 1 egg white. Break up the egg white with a palette knife and add the sugar a spoonful at a time. Beat it thoroughly by hand between each addition of sugar. A squeeze of lemon juice will help to give the icing a whiter appearance.

PASTILLAGE (1)

❖

This paste dries very hard.

250g (8 oz/1½ cups) sieved icing
(confectioners') sugar
15ml (1 tbsp) gum tragacanth, CMC or Tylose
5ml (1 tsp) liquid glucose (thick corn syrup)
25 – 30ml (5 – 6 tsp) cold water

Sift the icing sugar and gum tragacanth, CMC or Tylose together. Make a depression in the centre of the sugar and add the liquid glucose. Add the water and mix thoroughly. Wrap the paste up well and leave for 24 hours.

PASTILLAGE (2)

❖

This recipe makes a more elastic paste.

75g (2½ oz) egg white
500g (1 lb/3 cups) icing (confectioners') sugar,
sifted
45 ml (3 tbsp) Tylose, gum tragacanth or CMC
15ml (1 tbsp) white vegetable fat

Make up a royal icing with the egg white and sugar, then add Tylose and mix well. The mixture will immediately start to thicken. Turn it out onto a sugared board and knead the white fat into the paste. Wrap it up well, leave it for at least 24 hours and then knead it again. Add more icing sugar or some cornflour (cornstarch) if the paste appears at all sticky.

PASTILLAGE (3)

❖

This very elastic paste is good for draping.

500g (1 lb/3 cups) icing (confectioners')
sugar, sifted
15ml (1 tbsp) gum tragacanth or CMC
10ml (2 tsp) powdered gelatine
25ml (5 tsp) cold water
10ml (2 tsp) liquid glucose (clear corn syrup)
10ml (2 tsp) white vegetable fat
1 large egg white

Warm the sugar and gum tragacanth or CMC

in a large bowl over a saucepan of hot water. Cover the sugar, so that it does not form a crust. ◉ Sprinkle the gelatine over the water and set aside for about 30 minutes. Melt the liquid glucose, white vegetable fat and gelatine over very low heat. Once the sugar is warm, stir it on slow speed using an electric mixer. Add the liquid glucose mixture and the egg white. Turn machine onto maximum speed and beat for about 15 minutes. The longer and harder it is beaten, the whiter it will become.

GUM ARABIC GLUE

This is used for gluing soft pieces of paste together.

15ml (1 tbsp) water
5ml (1 tsp) gum arabic

◉ Measure the water into a small screw-topped jar and add the gum arabic. Shake well until the powder has dissolved. Store in the refrigerator.

GUMPASTE GLUE

This is used for gluing structural parts together.

175g (5½ oz) icing (confectioners') sugar, sifted
2.5ml (½ tsp) CMC, Tylose or gum tragacanth
30ml (2 tbsp) tepid water

Sift the sugar and gum tragacanth, CMC or Tylose together. Add the sifted mixture to water stirring all the time, then leave, covered, for about 1 hour before use.

MARBLING
≈

Marbling can create an effect like stone, varnished or roughly sawn wood, or natural elements such as sea or a cloudy sky. ◉ Colour paste with an appropriate base colour – for example, pale blue or turquoise for sea or sky. Then add a small amount of white or grey-coloured paste in lumps and knead together briefly; roll out. Because the pieces are only partially mixed, the lighter areas appear as streaks or blobs. By rolling and pulling the mixture in one direction only, you will obtain streaks; if you blend it by folding and rolling lengthways and sideways, you will obtain swirls and blobs.

MODELLING TOOLS

One of the best investments is a set of high-quality modelling tools. These are essential for delicate work, for indenting patterns, and for figures, flowers and other cake-top ornaments. Avoid badly made tools, especially those with a ridge where the moulded halves are joined as this may tear or scratch the paste.

FIGURE MOULDS

I prefer to mould figures - especially lightly clad ones – freehand because it is very difficult to remove the marks on the paste. For example, torsos for the fairies, see page 54, are moulded but the limbs are hand modelled. Many of the full figure moulds are too large to be practical for sugarcraft purposes.

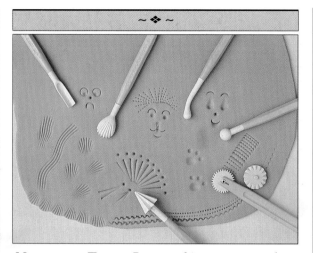

MODELLING TOOLS *Do not skimp on a good set of modelling tools. You will need all of them to create attractive-looking patterns. Either buy them as a set or obtain them individually as you need them.*

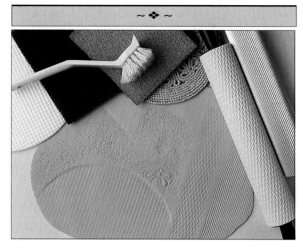

TEXTURING TOOLS *It is possible to improvise sugar modelling tools from ordinary domestic equipment and even items such as pieces of plastic packaging.*

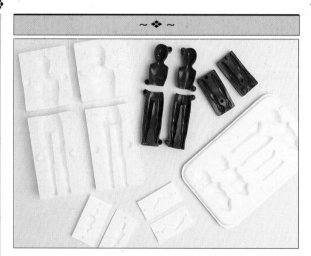

FIGURE MOULDS *Figure moulds are useful for heads, faces and limbs. You can form the other parts by hand because in most cases it is only necessary to create the general shape over which to apply layers of clothing.*

SHAPERS FOR PASTILLAGE *Bowls, pieces of plastic guttering, vacuum-formed chocolate trays and polythene bags can all be useful when modelling a variety of different items.*

MODELLING TECHNIQUES

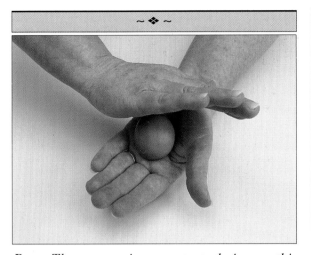

BALL The most important technique, this rolling action leaves the surface of the paste smooth. Place the paste in the palm of one hand. Lightly rest the other over it, cupping the hands together. Move the hands in a circular motion. Do not squeeze too hard.

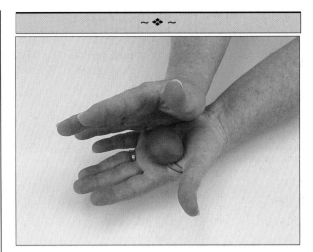

CONE To modify the ball into a cone shape, raise your fingers while bringing the sides of your hands together. Rub them from side to side, then up and down while gently squeezing the paste, and it will gradually change shape.

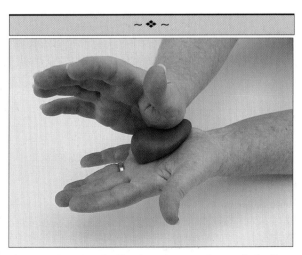

PEAR Place a ball of paste in the soft hollow between the base of the thumb and the heel of the hand. Place the other hand on top, with its heel slightly higher and gently rub your hands from side to side. Do not let your wrists touch, or the pear will be too thin at the narrow end.

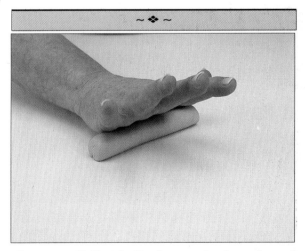

CYLINDER Roll a ball of paste backwards and forwards under the palm of the hand. Do not use your fingers. To make a thread-like ribbon, roll a cylinder between the work surface and an icing smoother. The paste will quickly extend as it is compressed by the smoother.

PROPORTIONS OF FIGURES

The diagrams show male and female figures against a grid of eight equally spaced segments. It is useful to know the simple rules which give realistic proportions. For example, the size of the adult head is about one-eighth of the height of the figure. The face, limbs and hands are the most important features. The hand is about the same length as the face, and the length of the head is half the width of the body at the shoulders. The distance from the knee to the ankle bone is roughly the same as that from the elbow to the knuckle; and the length of the foot is the same as the distance from the elbow to the wrist. The elbows are positioned at waist height when the arms are relaxed and the tips of the fingers reach almost halfway down the thighs. Children's proportions are slightly different, since their heads are relatively large compared with their bodies. Toddlers' heads are about one-fifth of their total height, whereas young teenagers' heads are about one-sixth of their height. Children's limbs are proportionally fatter than adults, but not so well muscled.

FACES The single most important feature. It is a good idea to maintain the accepted proportions: the centre of the ears halfway up the head; eyebrows line up with tops of the ears; earlobes in line with the base of the nose; mouth just above halfway point between nose and chin.

HANDS can be long oval shapes, with fingertips just extending beyond the end. When working on very small pieces, it is sufficient to create a

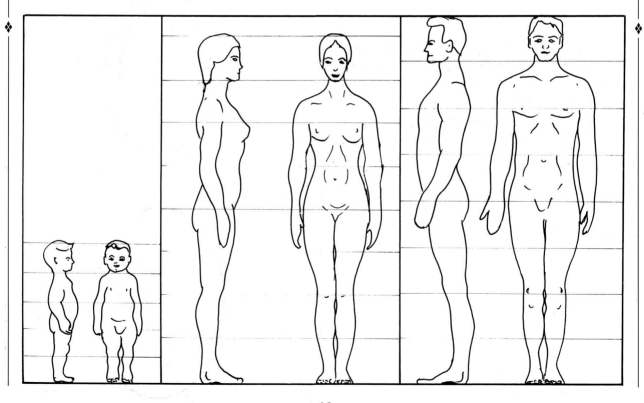

hand impression by snipping a 'V' section from the side of an oval piece of paste to leave a mitten shape. This separates the thumb from the fingers. If the oval is then cupped gently, the resulting shape looks similar to a relaxed hand.

FEET are about one and a half times bigger than hands. Women's feet are proportionally smaller than men's. Generally, sugar models are wearing shoes or boots, but if you intend a model to have bare feet, base the shape on a wedge, taper it at one end for the toes, and separate the big toe from the other four. Round the heel and shape the back of the foot to a gently radiused curve.

EXPERT ADVICE

≈

You can break any of these conventions on proportion when you decide to create special effects. Comic figures or toys often have extra large heads, feet and hands as you will see if you refer to the rag doll on page 38.

Proportions and Colour Features of Eyes

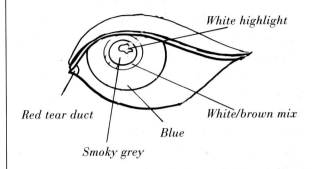

White highlight

Red tear duct

White/brown mix

Blue

Smoky grey

Detailed Hand – Proportions and Features

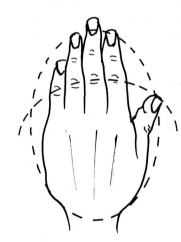

Mitten Hand

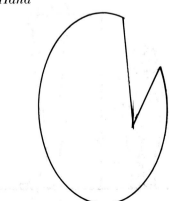

PAINTING EYES *Fill the sockets with white royal icing; dry. Paint on the pupil and iris. Do not make the iris a full circle or the eyes too bright, except for comic faces. Paint the pupil black or grey, leaving a white highlight. Outline round the whole eye and paint the eyelashes.*

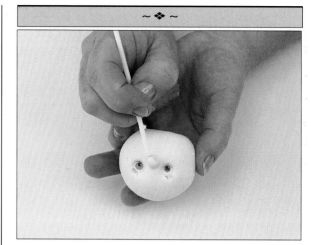

MAKING NOSES *Attach a ball of paste, smoothing it into position with a modelling stick or tool. Insert the rounded end of the modelling stick into the nose to define the nostrils; it may be turned up for a lady or hooked for a man.*

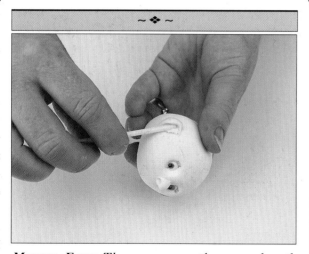

MAKING EARS *These measure the same length as the distance between the eyebrows and the base of the nose. Shape an oval of paste into a question mark, then attach it. Use a modelling stick to merge the top edge into the head. Cup the other edge around the stick for the lobe.*

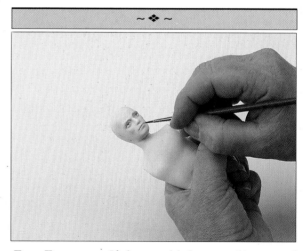

FINE FEATURES *If the mould does not have good definition, use hand modelling and painting skills to enhance facial features. The auger or veining tool is especially useful. Blend pink and brown colours for lips, and dusting powders to emphasize contours. Highlight with white.*

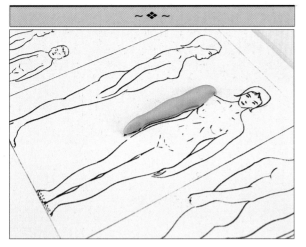

ARMS *Use the diagram on page 10. Roll a cylinder of skintone paste. Thin the wrist and elbow by rolling the paste between your index fingers, making a smaller indent for the elbow. Trim the top at an angle where the arm meets the shoulder to fit snugly against the body.*

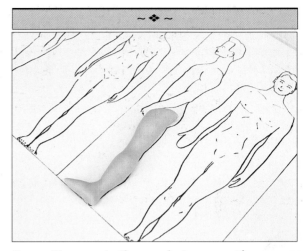

LEGS *Use a similar technique as for arms. Rotate the paste between your index fingers to thin it at the knee. The shinbone is straight and the calf muscle bulges at the back of the leg. Thin the ankle, and bend the foot at right angles. Trim the upper leg at an angle.*

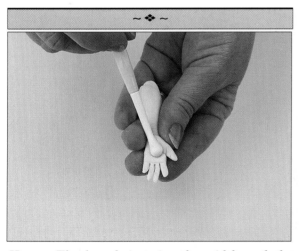

HANDS *The length is twice the width and the palm should be square. Cut a 'V' for the thumb to extend halfway up from the palm. Thin and snip four fingers; run a modelling stick between them and curve each to smooth the edges. Note the comparative lengths of fingers.*

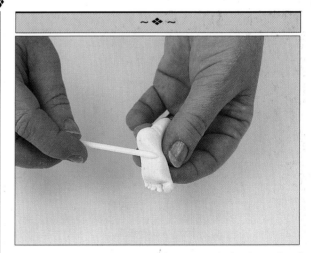

FEET *From heel to toe, they equal the length of the head and are wedge shaped: thicker and narrower at the heel than the toes. The inside edge is curved at the instep. The big toe is almost twice as thick as the others; it has one knuckle. The smaller toes have two knuckles.*

USING FIGURE MOULDS

Many different sorts of mould are available; some are well proportioned and have fine details but some will give very poor impressions. You can also make your own moulds from pastillage, dental plaster, which will give fine definitions, or from latex rubber. A toy doll can be used as a former. If making a latex mould, the rubber should be painted onto the figure in thin layers; it will take up to 15 layers to build up enough rubber to form a reasonable mould.

Two-part rigid plastic moulds are the easiest to obtain, but when using them, do not make the body in two halves and stick them together, or you will end up with poor joins. Instead press one piece of paste between the two halves of the moulds and cut away any excess paste.

❖ Grease each part of the mould with a very small amount of silicone-based release agent. This is preferable to a vegetable fat which may cause problems if you wish to paint the figure later on.

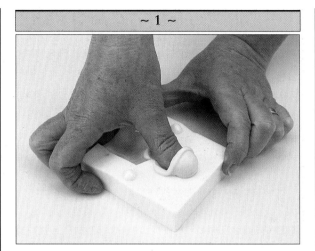

~ 1 ~

For a face, roll a ball of paste about half the diameter of the head. Press it hard – and once only – into the face of the mould. Trim off any excess paste from the neck, leaving only the face covered with paste.

~ 3 ~

Remove the back of the mould and trim any more excess paste. Re-position the mould and repeat this action two or three times, until all excess material is eliminated. Burnish the seam lines with an auger or veining tool. Do not remove the front of the mould yet.

~ 2 ~

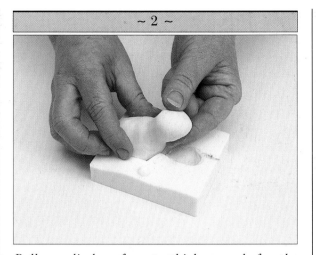

Roll a cylinder of paste thick enough for the body. Thin it for the neck, allowing it to bulge for the head back. Place in the mould, joining it to the paste in the face. Put the back of the mould on top and press very firmly, so that any excess paste is squeezed out.

~ 4 ~

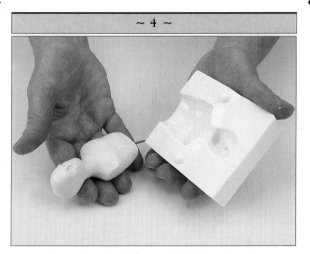

Insert a cocktail stick (toothpick) into the torso to lever the paste from the mould. Be careful not to distort the neck when releasing the head. While still soft, smooth the join lines. Insert the cocktail stick into a block of polystyrene to support the torso, incline the head and dry.

OBJECTS

We are surrounded by so many things competing for our attention that our senses become overloaded, and we often fail to observe what everyday objects really look like. Most of the time this doesn't matter, because experience reassures us that we actually do know, for example, what the surface of a brick is like, or how big it is compared with other commonplace items. To be successful with modelling, we have to examine the object we wish to reproduce, and distil its essential outline from its overall appearance. It is impossible to reproduce an exact replica of something made from wood, stone, metal or flesh and blood.

Begin by consciously looking at the most apparent qualities of the object. If, for example, it is a man's shoe, decide if it is really solid black, or is it actually dark blue with highlights of white or pale grey. Consider its size relative to the things surrounding it, and its finish – is it shiny, or matt, does it look heavy or is it delicate? If it is very intricate, like the carvings on an old church, can you see any general pattern in the stones which could be reproduced easily?

After you have considered these points, use the information you have gleaned to create your model. If you are using a mould, you will have less freedom to express your own ideas, but if you are working freehand, you can interpret them to create a figure or object that is as realistic as possible, comic or fantastic. To illustrate this point, look at the figures used in the finished designs: soldiers on the fort, sailors in the dingy and the man kneeling in the Victorian tableau. Two of these examples are comic in appearance, but they are all carefully proportioned, accurately shaped to reflect the actions which they are performing, and use colours which help to explain their purpose. Two of the three figures, even though in proportion, are no more anatomically correct than the rag doll on page 38 but this does not detract from their effectiveness.

Because pastillage is brittle after it has hardened, it is more difficult to work than most other modelling materials. Therefore the easiest way to assemble complicated models would therefore seem to be to make their individual pieces so accurately that they fit together without further adjustment. In practice this is difficult because as pastillage dries out, it also shrinks slightly, and some trimming is often required to achieve accurate joins, especially where flat thin sections like walls and frames are concerned.

The following methods work well:

◉ For straight edges, use a fine grade of emery paper (150 grit), and lay it flat on your worktop. Hold the hardened piece of paste as close to the edge needing to be trimmed, as possible, then rub it on the abrasive surface. Rub along the edge to be trimmed, not across it.

◉ For curves, wrap the abrasive paper over a former, then gently brush the pastillage against it, rubbing along the edge which needs trimming, not across the edge.

◉ Flat surfaces will tolerate a little polishing to remove minor blemishes, but large-scale sanding to modify shapes is very difficult as the paste tends to snap.

Where more complicated mouldings like the upper edges of a boat hull require sanding, proceed very slowly and delicately. Place the piece in the centre of a fresh sheet of emery paper and rub it lightly in a circular motion. Do not let it move off the sheet, as there is a risk that the piece will catch on the edge, and snap.

When very small adjustments to an edge are needed, try using a manicure emery board or nail buffer as a file. In all cases, keep the abrasive from clogging by blowing the sugar dust from its surface after every dozen or so strokes.

Sometimes it is necessary to make a hole through a piece of hardened paste, and although it is possible to drill it, the easier, if slightly messier, method is to heat a metal skewer in a gas flame or on an electric hotplate, and burn out the hole. However, this leaves a deposit of burned and blackened sugar around the rim of the hole, which may have to be sanded off.

STEAMING The gums used in some pastillage recipes are tolerant of moist heat, and therefore it is sometimes possible to introduce curves into a flat piece of pastillage by steaming the area to be bent. However, when the pastillage has re-hardened, it is usually much weaker in that area.

REINFORCING Models with long, spindly necks or legs can be reinforced by passing a piece of dowel, a satay stick or cocktail stick (toothpick), or a piece of wire through them while the pastillage is still pliable, and then leaving the reinforcing material in the item after the paste has dried. This of course makes the models inedible. The figures in the tableau on page 61 are both reinforced in this way using satay sticks, which were deliberately left to protrude from the model so that they could be pressed into the icing base of the tableau to give the figures stability.

If a large model is clearly not intended for consumption, it is also possible to reinforce it permanently with wedges made from small pieces of polystyrene, which may be stuck in place with royal icing.

GLUING There are three principal methods of joining pieces of pastillage:

Royal Icing This is ideal for large and relatively heavy areas, such as the panels of pastillage representing the walls of a building.

Gumpaste Glue Mix a small quantity of fresh pastillage with gum arabic glue or egg white to make a sticky paste of the consistency of syrup or honey. This is especially useful for joining objects of the same colour, as you can make it up from a leftover piece of coloured pastillage. It is ideal, for example, for gluing items like arms and legs in position.

Gum Arabic Glue Used as a liquid glue, this is ideal for joining small and very fragile pieces, especially for items such as clothing or delicate frills.

STRENGTH AND DURABILITY Food colourings in general have extremely poor lightfastness, and are particularly susceptible to fading when exposed to sunlight. Violets and reds fade faster than yellows, but even black will lose its

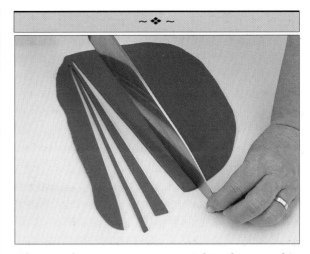

The simplest way to cut straight edges or thin strips of pastillage is by using a long-bladed kitchen knife. Place the tip on the work surface at the edge of the pastillage and then lower the blade with a guillotining action. This prevents the knife from dragging through the paste and making it stretch or distort.

intensity after two weeks of strong direct sunlight. Keep your models in a shaded area, or better still in a dark cupboard. Varnishing a model with confectioners' glaze may help, and this does strengthen the pastillage, particularly if several layers are applied.

If possible when drying pieces of pastillage, lay them on unvarnished wood, foam sponge or teflon-coated matting. After the pastillage has dried sufficiently to handle, turn the pieces over. You will see that the paste is darker in the areas where it is still moist. Turning the pieces over will prevent the paste from warping.

EXPERT ADVICE
≈

Caution should be exercised in the use of inedible reinforcements, since it is important not to lose sight of the objective of making items from sugar. Obviously there must be a point at which a model can no longer be defined as a sugar model if it contains an excessive amount of foreign non-sugar reinforcing matter.

FINISHES AND TEXTURES

❖

Many of the textures and finishes used in this book have been obtained by using everyday household equipment, including that shown on page 8. The techniques are explained in detail here to avoid repetition later.

WOODGRAIN This is a specialized form of marbling. Knead light brown food colouring into a ball of sugarpaste or pastillage until it is almost fully dispersed, then wipe the ball with a cocktail stick (toothpick) which has been dipped in dark brown or black colouring. Stretch the paste and fold the ends into the streaks. Stretch it and fold it again, then roll it out thinly. The streaks of colour will appear on the surface of the paste as a random pattern of dark lines against a lighter background.

GRASS Grass can be made in a variety of ways – for larger areas use a scourer or washing-up brush to indent the soft sugarpaste. For strands of grass or hair, roll out a small piece of pastillage until it is wafer-thin and about 2.5cm (1 in) wide by 7.5cm (3 in) long, then fringe one edge. Clumps of coarse grass can be made by pushing lumps of sugarpaste through a fine wire sieve, and removing with a palette knife. Stick the tufts and clumps in place with Gum Arabic Glue, see page 7.

EXPERT ADVICE

≈

An effective metallic 'paint' can be made by mixing lustre or sparkle dusting powders (petal dusts/blossom tints) with edible confectioners' glaze. This mixture was used on the top of the mushroom on page 56.

BARK The bark of logs and trees is made when the pastillage is soft. Use a fine-pointed scriber, a pin, or a wire modelling brush to score the pastillage. Mark the surface roughly, keeping the scratch lines going in the same general direction but occasionally swirling the scratches so that they look like a wood knot, or a place where a branch has been removed. When the pastillage has dried, paint it with a mixture of dark brown, chestnut and moss green colouring.

BRICKWORK Roll out a piece of pastillage, and with the edge of a ruler or straight edge, indent it with a series of regularly spaced parallel lines. This creates the courses or rows of bricks. Use a small modelling tool to make vertical lines along the courses to mark the ends of individual bricks. Finish as shown right.

SAND AND GRAVEL Rolled-out cream coloured pastillage is patted with a heavy-duty scourer or washing-up brush until the surface is evenly marked. Sprinkle it with ground almonds, semolina, yellow and brown sugartex, or brown sugar crystals.

PEBBLES Take pieces of black, brown, white, green and a tiny amount of blue and violet sugarpaste or pastillage and break them into small pieces about the size of pea. Press into one ball but do not knead. This is a useful way of using up leftover pieces of pastillage, for the pebbles will keep indefinitely once glazed.

STONEWORK Roll out a piece of grey-coloured pastillage and marble it using dull colourings such as black, dark brown or green. Indent the outlines of the individual stones with a straight edge by pressing it into the soft paste. Make the vertical lines using a shell/blade modelling knife (not a sharp craft knife). Then define the corners of stones by dragging the point of the modelling knife around each one.

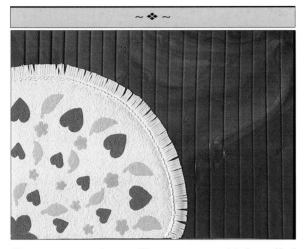

For carpet and towelling, texture thinly rolled coloured pastillage by patting it firmly with a stiff washing-up brush. Pat the surface with the brush until it has a regular pitted appearance.

For grass, cut a fine fringe along one edge of a thin pastillage strip, leaving about 5mm (¼ in) uncut on the other edge. Roll it up carefully to form tufts of long grass, or alternatively leave it as a strip.

For bricks, pipe cream or light brown royal icing into the grooves for the mortar. Brush with a damp paintbrush to smooth the icing into the lines of indentation. Sand and Gravel, see left.

For pebbles, break off small pieces or crumbs of the unkneaded pastillage. Roll them into balls and then shape them to form tiny pebbles. When dry, dip them in confectioners' glaze and leave to harden. Stonework, see left.

PERSPECTIVE

❖

If you plan to make models of large objects, like the fort on page 23 or the tableau on page 61, it is useful to have a knowledge of the basic rules of perspective. They will help you to decide whether to adjust your templates in order to strengthen the illusion of distance between the closest and furthest points, and to establish the correct relationship between the size of the objects in the background and foreground.

DISTORTING SIZES TO CREATE DISTANCE
Perspective distorts the size of objects to make them appear smaller the further away they are. If you imagine a scene where you are standing in front of a building, the front seems bigger than the back (see diagram opposite), and if you could project straight lines from its edges, away from you towards some distant horizon, all the lines would eventually converge at what is called the vanishing point. All the other objects you see in that same scene also have a vanishing point somewhere along the same horizon, regardless of their size.

CHANGING THE VIEWPOINT If in your imagination you walk a little way to the right and position yourself at the corner of the building, your viewpoint will be different, and the place where the imaginary lines would converge will also have moved, but it will still be on the same horizon. Moreover, if you could extend another set of imaginary lines from the building, away to the left, they would also converge at the horizon, but at the left-hand side of the building. The front of the building would appear shorter, and the side would seem longer, because from your new position you could see more of one and less of the other.

This rule applies to all objects and even though they may not conveniently arrange themselves along the imaginary lines extending from the closest building or person, their vanishing points will always converge at the horizon. You can use these imaginary lines to help you to scale objects to the right size.

FIGURES IN PERSPECTIVE In the diagram, the matchstick figure no. 1 was drawn first. Then figure no. 2 was drawn by extending parallel lines horizontally from the converging lines linking the first figure to the horizon. Finally figure no. 3 was added, closest to the viewer, and proportioned using the original set of converging lines. If they could be moved, and paraded shoulder to shoulder, the figures would be of equal height. The actual difference in the sizes on the diagram is solely the effect of perspective.

EXPERT ADVICE
≈

If you want to make a tableau of a scene arranged inside a room, use the rules of perspective to help to give it depth. Imagine that you are looking onto a stage and there is a wall facing you with another to the left and another to the right. Build the tableau with the side walls placed at the angles illustrated, and construct the left- and right-hand walls using the shapes of 'A' and 'B' with their longest edge towards you, see templates on page 59.

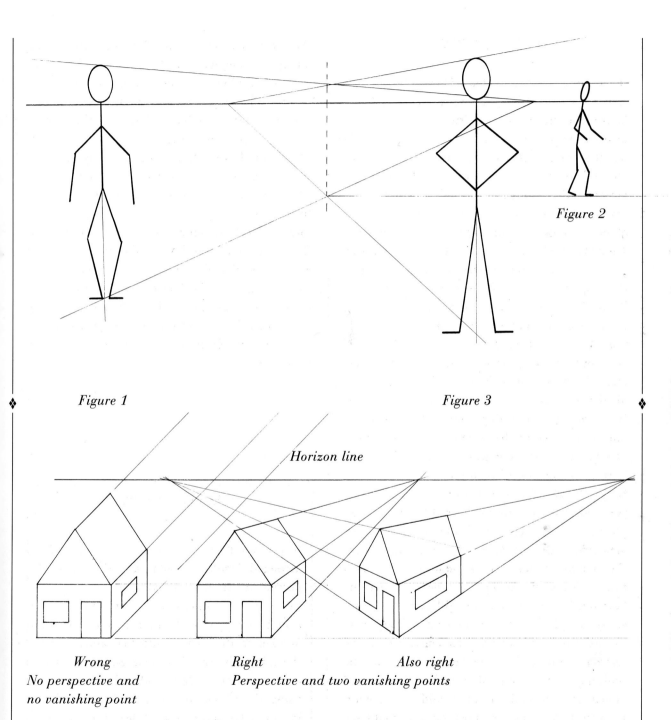

Figure 2

Figure 1

Figure 3

Horizon line

Wrong
No perspective and
no vanishing point

Right
Perspective and two vanishing points

Also right

FORT CAKE

25cm (10 in) square cake
20cm (8 in) square cake
1.75kg (3½ lb) marzipan (almond paste)
3kg (6 lb) sugarpaste
apricot glaze or buttercream
selection of paste and dusting powder (petal
dust/blossom tint) food colourings
250g (8 oz) Pastillage (1), see page 6
60g (2 oz) Pastillage (2 or 3), see page 6
small amount of royal icing
Gumpaste Glue, see page 7
piping gel
Gum Arabic Glue, see page 7

EQUIPMENT

25cm (10 in) square cake board
45cm (18 in) square cakeboard
paper glue ● polystyrene blocks
modelling tools ● no. 0 piping tube (tip)
parchment triangles
wooden cocktail sticks (toothpicks)
gold lustre

● Start by making the pastillage battlements, the drawbridge and the castle entrance using the templates on page 66, so that they can dry while the rest of the cake is being prepared. For this kind of construction, use Pastillage (1), a hard-drying paste. For the battlements and drawbridge, the paste should be about 3mm (⅛ in) thick, but for the door and its fittings, it can be 1 or 2mm (⅟₃₂ or ⅟₁₆ in) thick. Indent the stonework pattern in the battlements, and the lines marking the planking of the wooden drawbridge, as described on page 25. Allow the paste to harden for 24 hours, turning the pieces over occasionally, so that they dry evenly from both sides.

● Trim the cakes so that they are flat. Cut the smaller one according to the diagram, see page 24, and use apricot glaze or buttercream to stick the four 20cm (8 in) sections to the top of the larger cake.

● Roll out a piece of the marbled sugarpaste to make an 18cm (7 in) square. Smooth it into place in the inset centre section of the top. Drape the whole cake with a large sheet of marbled sugarpaste. Cut an opening carefully in the exact centre and then trim and stretch it until it fits against the inner part of the walls surrounding the 18cm (7 in) inset square. Finally, finish smoothing the sugarpaste against the sides of the cake. Make sure that the coating is even, as it is the foundation to which the pastillage battlements will later be attached.

● While the sugarpaste is soft, indent it with lines to represent the courses of stonework, then indent the vertical lines to separate the individual blocks. Cover the four 5cm (2 in) squares of cake and stick these onto the corners.

● Prepare the base for the cake by sticking the two cake boards together using paper glue. Arrange them as shown in the diagram on page 24. Coat the boards with a single piece of green-coloured sugarpaste, then remove the sugarpaste from the 'L'-shaped part which will form the moat. Use this piece to build up the level of the bank along the edges of the larger board. Lay some blue sugarpaste in the bottom of the moat. Set the cake in place on the smaller board and add the battlements, using royal icing to secure them and holding them in place with foam blocks or polystyrene scraps until they are set. Patch up any cracks with coloured royal icing or gumpaste glue. Spread piping gel over the moat, position the drawbridge and attach the wood and stonework entrance.

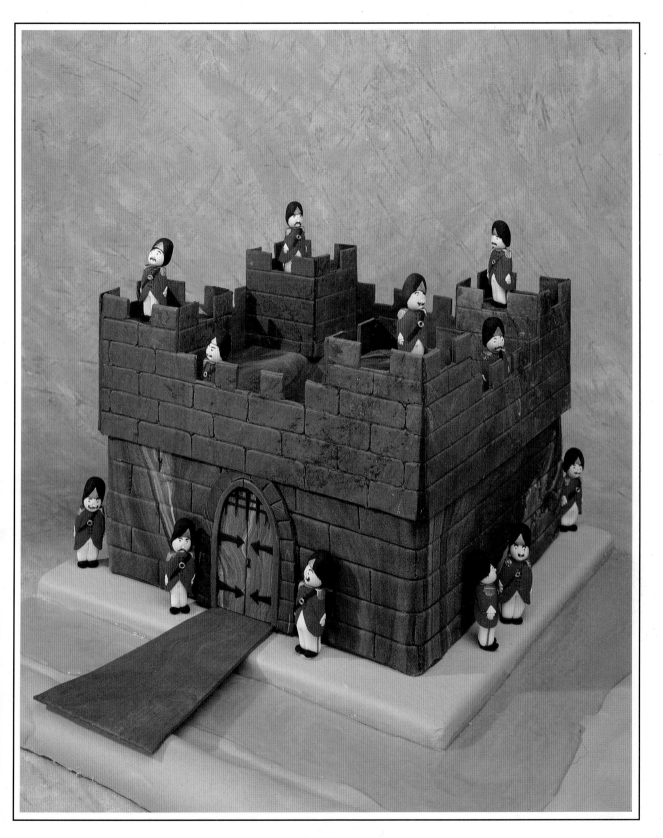

THE SOLDIERS

❖

The red-uniformed guards should be mass produced as about a dozen are needed. Pastillage (2) or (3) may be used for these. Make the head. Fill the eye sockets with white royal icing and, when dry, paint a black dot for the eyes, the details of the eyebrows and moustaches.

The body of each soldier is made from a 7g (¼ oz) piece of pastillage, see right. Impress a groove down each side of the upper body to suggest the outline of the arms. Insert a cocktail stick into the base of each body, and use it to stand each one in a block of polystyrene until it has hardened.

Make the trouser features and jacket, see right. Mould the sides of the jacket carefully against the grooves delineating the arms. Mark a row of indentations for the tunic buttons with the pointed end of a modelling stick. Pipe with dots of royal icing when dry.

Make the hands from tiny discs of skin-coloured paste. Cut a 'V' to separate the thumb, then glue the hands to the ends of the arms. Cut a small diamond of white paste in half and stick one half to the cuff of each sleeve.

Make the clothing features, see right. When dry, join the heads to the bodies with a small collar of soft blue paste. Paint the shoulder tabs, tunic, buckle, cuffs and front of the bearskin with gold lustre. Remove the cocktail stick, join the feet to the body with black royal icing and place on the fort.

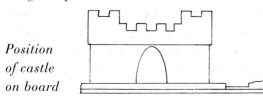

*Position
of castle
on board*

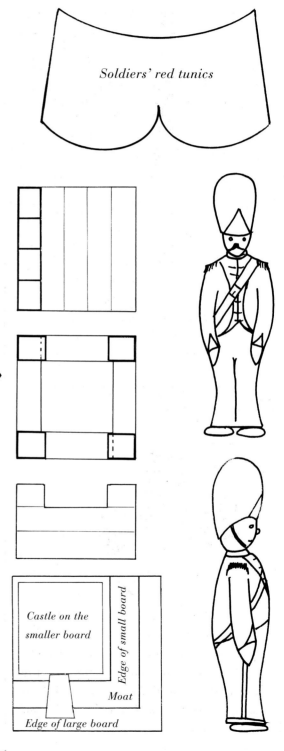

Soldiers' red tunics

*Castle on the
smaller board*

Edge of small board

Moat

Edge of large board

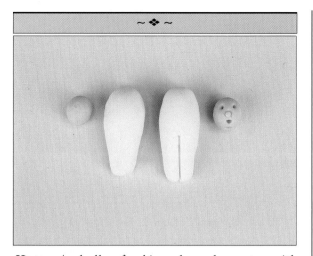

HEAD *A ball of skin-coloured paste with indented eyes, mouth and nose. A tiny part-squashed carrot-shaped piece of paste makes the nose.* **BODY** *Elongated and flattened paste, indented to form legs with shallow side grooves for trouser seams.*

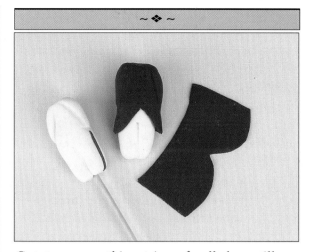

Cut two very thin strips of rolled pastillage. Paint the lines on the trouser legs with gum arabic glue and insert the blue paste to form stripes. Cut out tunic from red paste, see page 24. Wrap the tunic around the hardened body so that the join line is at the back.

Make a strap from pastillage. Roll a tiny ball of paste and attach this to look like a buckle. Make shoulder tabs from small cones of white paste, indented to form the braids. Mould a black ball of paste to look like a bearskin and stick it to the head.

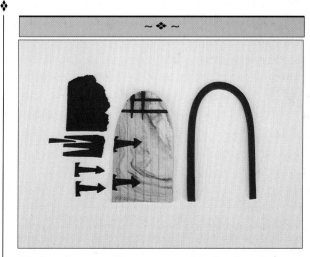

Make the pastillage gate. Mark the door to simulate planking. Cut out and assemble the black portcullis, hinges and door frame while the door is flat, then stick to the cake with dark grey gumpaste glue or royal icing. Mould the stone archway around the door frame.

PENGUIN POOL

30 x 25cm (12 x 10 in) oval cake
875g (1¾ lb) marzipan (almond paste)
1.5kg (3 lb) sugarpaste ● apricot glaze
selection of paste and dusting powder (petal dust/blossom tint) food colourings
500g (1 lb) Pastillage (1), see page 6
small amount of royal icing
Gum Arabic Glue, see page 7
Gumpaste Glue, see page 7
piping gel
EQUIPMENT
36 x 30cm (14 x 12 in) oval cakeboard
no. 32 plain 26mm scallop crimper
teflon-coated cloth ● small ball tool
shell modelling tool ● polystyrene blocks
wooden cocktail sticks (toothpicks)
confectioners' glaze

● Coat the cake with marzipan and turquoise-coloured sugarpaste. Cover the board and trim the edge with the scallop crimper. Set aside for 24 hours until the icing is hard. Meanwhile, make the pastillage decorations. Roll out the pastillage for the edge of the pool to a thickness of about 5mm (¼ in). Cut an oval-shaped piece of paste and use the template on page 28 as a guide when cutting away the centre section. Leave the piece to dry thoroughly. Stick it to the top of the cake with royal icing.

● Roll out the pastillage for the icebergs to a thickness of about 2mm (⅟₁₆ in). Cut out the jagged iceberg shapes using the templates, see below. Stand a cake tin on its edge, and drape the pieces of paste around both the inside and outside of the tin so that they set in a curve. Use strips of teflon-coated cloth attached to the tin to prevent the icebergs sticking. Leave to harden for about 24 hours.

● When the icebergs are dry, dust them with pale blue and green dusting powder. Use a mask made from paper or thin card to prevent any stray colour from blurring the edges of the pattern. Set the pieces in place using royal icing.

PENGUINS

● Roll a 30g (1 oz) ball of equal quantities of pastillage and sugarpaste into a pear shape. Pinch and bend the narrow end for the neck and beak, see right. Indent the eye sockets with a small ball tool.

Iceberg templates

Paint the body. When the black has dried, paint the beak a deep orange. Make the feet from a kidney-shaped piece of orange paste, marked with a shell modelling tool. Stick the bird directly onto the paste.

Follow the steps, right, to make the slide. Make the diving board from a strip of pastillage, dried in a slight curve, and then joined to two cylinders of paste with royal icing.

The penguin about to spring into the water is glued in place with icing. Spread the pool with a thin layer of piping gel and position the penguins.

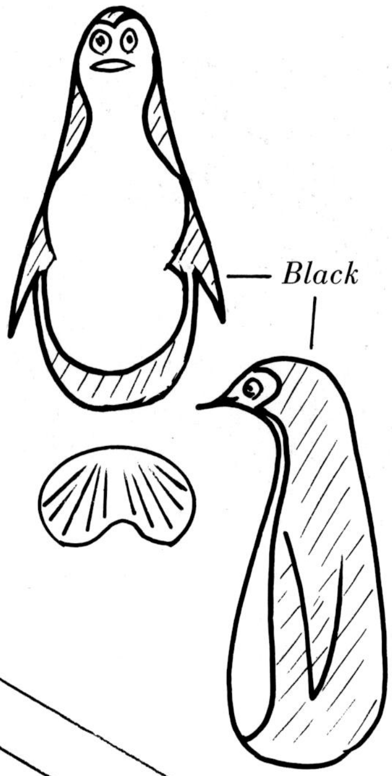

Black

Diving Board

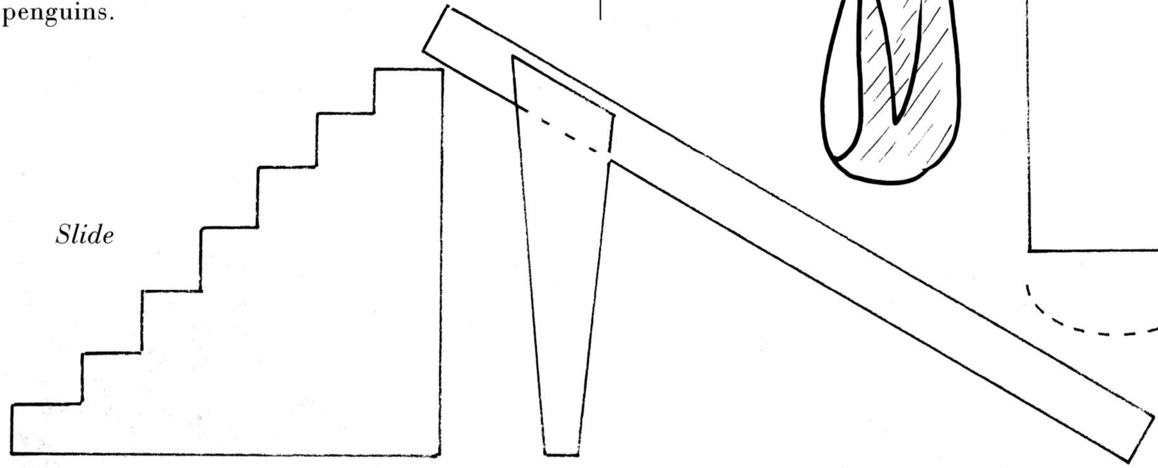

Slide

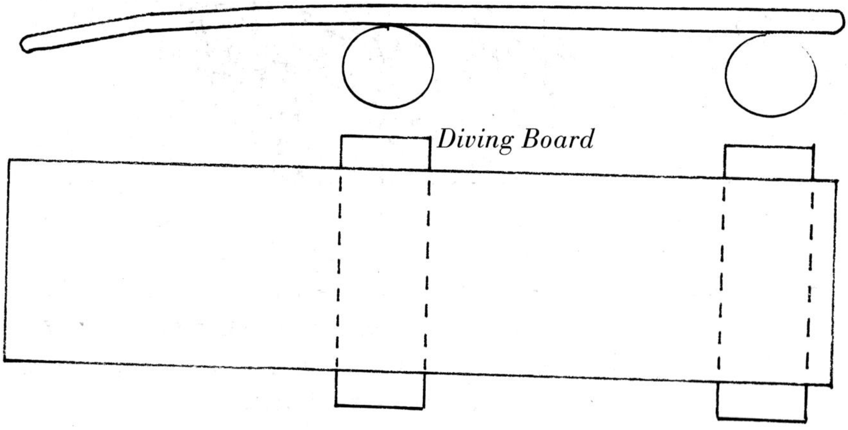

Pool Outline

Diving Board

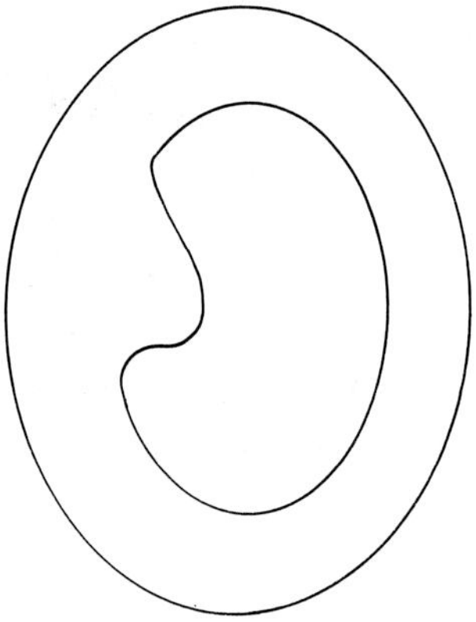

~ 1 ~

Use a pair of nail scissors to snip each side of the body to form the penguins' flippers. Bend them away from the body and arrange the bird in the required posture. Leave to harden for 24 hours.

~ 2 ~

Paint strong black food colouring with only a minimum of dilution over the back and down the flippers, being careful to avoid smudging the bird's white chest.

~ 3 ~

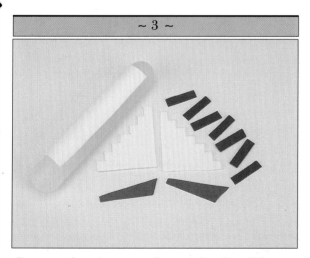

Cut out the pieces used to make the slide, see page 28. Use a small rolling pin or a piece of dowelling as a former to curve the chute until it hardens.

~ 4 ~

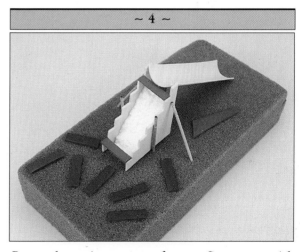

Rest the pieces on foam. Support with polystyrene and cocktail sticks (toothpicks); stick the treads to the sides first, then add the chute. The tapered legs support the top of the chute. One is already in place while the other lies behind the cocktail stick.

THE SEASIDE CAKE

*A*rches under a seaside promenade often house piles of deckchairs or mysterious pieces of abandoned and rusting fishing gear. Sometimes they provide access to the town beyond. On this almost deserted stretch of beach, only one holiday-maker remains, oblivious to the encroaching tide.

25cm (10 in) square cake
apricot glaze or piping gel
1kg (2 lb) marzipan (almond paste)
1.5kg (3 lb) sugarpaste
selection of paste and dusting powder (petal dust/blossom tint) food colourings
piping gel
small amount of royal icing
250g (8 oz) Pastillage (1), see page 6
125g (4 oz) Pastillage (2), see page 6
Gum Arabic Glue, see page 7
small amount of ground almonds
EQUIPMENT
45 x 30cm (18 x 12 in) rectangular cake board
no. 14 mini open double scallop crimper
no. 0 piping tube (tip)
parchment triangles ● small star cutter
set of round cutters ● umbrella mould
small plastic funnel ● food colouring pens
plastic playing card ● polystyrene blocks

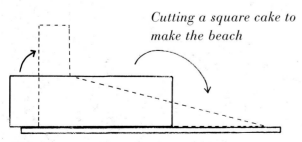

Cutting a square cake to make the beach

Side view – outline of cake on board

● Cut a 5cm (2 in) section from one end of the cake, then cut a section out of one side and arrange the pieces as shown in the diagram below left. Join the edges with apricot glaze or piping gel and cover with marzipan.

● Place the cake on a rectangular board. Cover the rear part with cream-coloured sugarpaste. Mix the remaining cream-coloured sugarpaste with the rest of the marzipan – the almonds will help give a textured effect to the sand.

● To make the sleeping sunbather, roll a little cylinder of sugarpaste, tapered at one end, and lay it in position on the marzipan before coating the beach section of the cake. Using the sugarpaste and marzipan mixture for the sand: colour it yellow and texture it as described on page 18. Use the feet of a small plastic doll to make the footprints in the sand.

● Make the sea by marbling some blue sugarpaste and applying a thin layer over the front edge of the board and the cake. Then roll the blue sugarpaste of the sea into the yellow of the sand so that the join is smooth at the water's edge. Apply a thick, irregular layer of piping gel to the blue sugarpaste to enhance the watery effect. Disguise the ridge at the point where the cake meets the board with clumps of seaweed, pebbles and stones.

● Roll out 250g (8 oz) of pastillage to a thickness of 4mm (³⁄₁₆ in), and use the template on page 66 to make the promenade facade. Set aside to dry for 48 hours. Paint the border and curved edges of the facade with brown food colouring. Mark their positions on the cake, then paint up to these marks with dark brown or black food colouring to create an illusion of deep shadow beneath each arch.

● Use royal icing to stick the facade to the front of the cake and retouch any parts of paint, if

necessary. Remember to paint the edges of the arches. Dab dark brown or black powder colouring onto the yellow paste at the base of the facade, to blur the join where the yellow paste used for the beach meets the cream paste of the promenade.

● Trim the upper edge of the facade with a strip of cream-coloured pastillage that has been crimped and then painted to represent a balcony rail along the edge of the promenade.

● Make the head of the sleeping sunbather from a ball of pastillage and pipe the sunglasses, nose and mouth. Cut a thin disc of pastillage, frill the edge and stick it to the head with gum arabic glue; then place it in position on the beach. Mould the feet and stick them into place. Add other embellishments, including the starfish, cut with a small star-shaped cutter, and the bucket and spade which are set in place after the sugarpaste has been sprinkled with ground almonds.

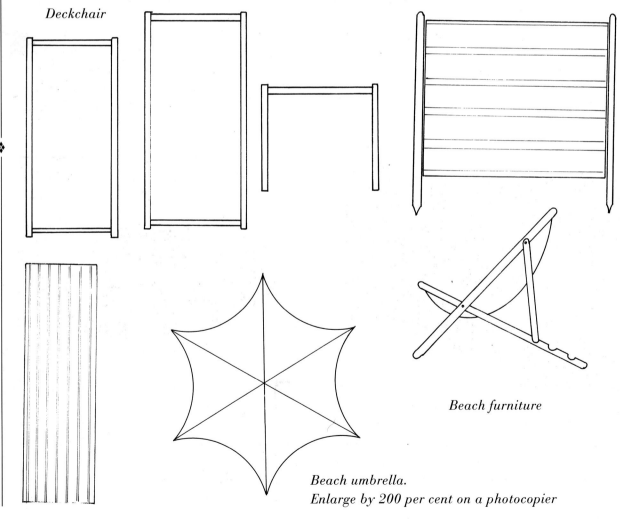

Deckchair

Windbreak

Beach furniture

Beach umbrella.
Enlarge by 200 per cent on a photocopier

~ 1 ~

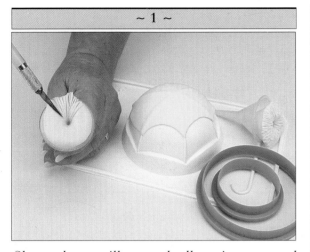

Shape the pastillage umbrella using a round cutter and a smaller one to indent the edge. Set over an umbrella mould or tennis ball. Mould the sunshade in a cone-shaped funnel and score with a craft knife. Dry. For the thatch, wrap fringes of paste around the outside.

~ 2 ~

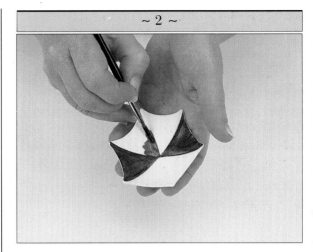

When the umbrella has hardened, remove it from its former and decorate it by painting the segments both inside and outside with red, green and yellow food colouring. Make the umbrella ribs from thin cylinders of pastillage.

~ 3 ~

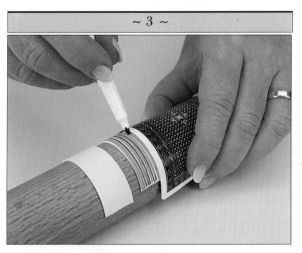

Make the canvas for deckchair and windbreak from thinly rolled pastillage and allow to set over a large rolling pin. Use food colouring pens to decorate it. A flexible plastic playing card is a useful guide for marking the straight lines as it will bend around the rolling pin.

~ 4 ~

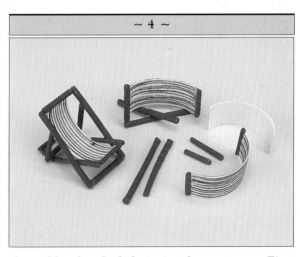

Assemble the deckchair in three stages. First stick the end pieces to the chair back, then join each of the pieces of one side, and when the joints have set, add the other side. Support the chair on a pad of foam until it is ready to be placed on the cake.

TOYBOX

An aeroplane, a rag doll, a wooden soldier, a skipping rope and a toy tank suggest that this traditional toybox is shared by a brother and sister. My own children were rarely as tidy as these two – their toys were kept all round the toybox, never actually in it!

20 x 13cm (8 x 5 in) cake
500g (1 lb) marzipan (almond paste)
2.5kg (5 lb) sugarpaste
apricot glaze
selection of paste and dusting powder (petal dust/blossom tint)
food colourings
small amount of royal icing
1 kg (2 lb) Pastillage (1), see page 6
500g (1 lb) Pastillage (2) or (3), see page 6
Gum Arabic Glue, see page 7
Gumpaste Glue, see page 7

EQUIPMENT

36 x 25cm (14 x 10 in) rectangular thin cake board
25 x 15cm (10 x 6 in) rectangular thin cake board
nos. 43c, 2, and 1.5 piping tubes (tips)
scriber ● parchment triangles
confectioners' glaze
no. 1 sable paintbrush ● small ball tool
blossom, heart and leaf cutters
no. 32 plain scallop crimper
no. 13 mini shut scallop crimper
Garrett frill cutter ● set of round cutters
polystyrene blocks

● Coat the cake with marzipan and cover it with pink sugarpaste. Cover the larger board with brown sugarpaste floorboards and make the carpet using the technique described on page 19. The toybox cake is supported on the smaller cakeboard, which is coated with green pastillage to match the colour of the frame.

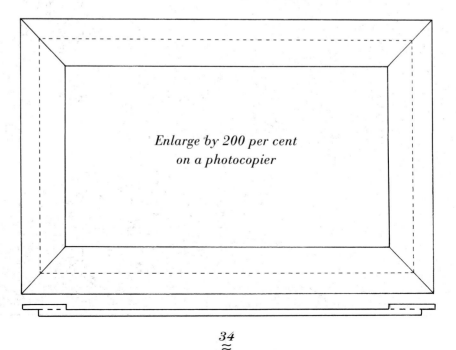

Enlarge by 200 per cent
on a photocopier

Use the templates below as a guide for cutting the side frames for the box and when the pastillage has dried, pipe a pattern of scrolls using a no. 43c piping tube (tip) – the remaining decorations are made with the writing tubes (tips). Before fixing the frame to the cake, mark the word 'TOYS' onto the front, and paint the letters with white dusting powder and confectioners' glaze using a no. 1 sable paintbrush. Roll out a rectangle of the pink pastillage for the toybox lid, see page 34, and leave to dry thoroughly for 48 hours before decorating it with its green frame. Also make two feet for the box 10cm (4 in) long x 1cm (½ in) thick.

MAKING THE TOYS

❖

Each of the toys is made from a mixture of equal quantities of sugarpaste and pastillage. Details for making the toy soldier are given on page 24. Note that the one shown here is approximately twice as large. To fill any of the space between the main toys, use up any coloured pieces of sugarpaste to make books, part of a ball or bits of broken toys.

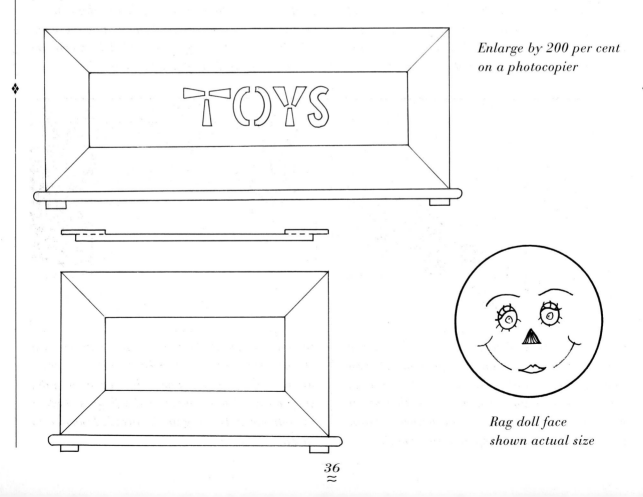

Enlarge by 200 per cent on a photocopier

Rag doll face shown actual size

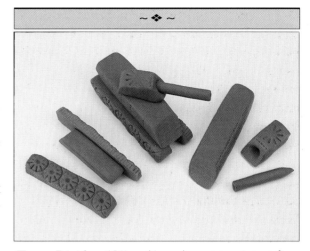

TEDDY BEAR *Use 60g (2 oz) paste to form one large and one small pear shape: the large for the body; small for the head. Divide 30g (1 oz) paste into quarters and roll into cylinders for limbs. Indent a tiny ball of paste for each ear. Use royal icing for eyes and details on feet.*

TANK *Divide 125g (4 oz) paste into five, following shapes shown on page 68. Emboss patterns onto the pieces to indicate the wheels, tracks and plating. Support the body on a block of leftover paste scraps concealed between the tracks. Dry for 24 hours before assembly.*

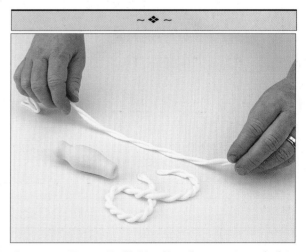

PLANE *Cut pieces of paste: 60g (2 oz) and 30g (1 oz). Roll larger into pear shape, elongate and taper narrower end, then squash to form an oval in cross section. Make wing with smaller piece, dry on a curve. Colour leftover scraps and use for windows, propeller and wheels.*

SKIPPING ROPE *Roll 60g (2 oz) paste into a thin strand. Double it and twist it into a braid. Allow 45g (1½ oz) paste for each handle, shaping a cylinder between the fingers. Indent the narrow ends and glue the braided paste into them.*

~ 1 ~

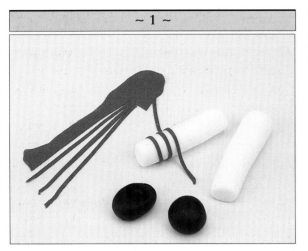

THE RAG DOLL: LEGS AND FEET *Two 30g (1 oz) cylinders of white paste wrapped with six wafer-thin strips of red paste make the legs. Black paste, rolled into an elongated ball and indented on one side, makes shoes, which are glued to the leg.*

~ 2 ~

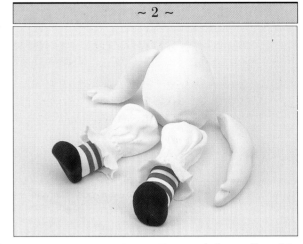

PANTALOONS AND BODY *For each leg roll a thin 10 x 5cm (4 x 2in) rectangle of paste. Frill one long side and wrap around knee. Gather and pleat the rest and secure it to the leg top. Make a ball of 100g (3½ oz) paste for the body. Shape 22g (¾ oz) skin-coloured paste for each arm.*

~ 3 ~

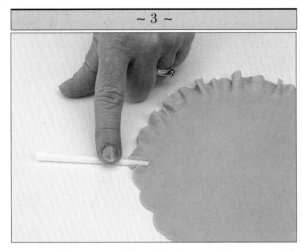

DRESS *Cut a scalloped edge with a no. 32 crimper on an 18cm (7 in) circle. Frill border; mark with mini crimper and drape over body. Make sleeves as for pantaloons. Trim dress neck with frilled and crimped paste circle. Add paste ribbons and bows on sleeves and neck.*

~ 4 ~

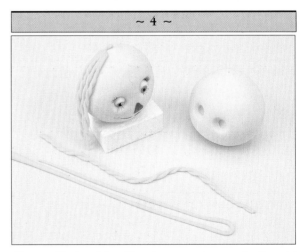

HEAD *Shape 90g (3 oz) paste into a ball, add the features and dry. Make the hair, see page 18, and work around the head, overlapping the strands to cover the back and sides. Add a tiny paste bow to conceal the parting along the head top.*

SAILING DINGHY

25cm (10 in) round cake
1kg (2 lb) marzipan (almond paste)
1.5kg (3 lb) sugarpaste ● apricot glaze
selection of paste and dusting powder (petal
dust/blossom tint) food colourings
small amount of royal icing
250g (8 oz) Pastillage (1), see page 6
125g (4 oz) Pastillage (2) or (3), see page 6
Gum Arabic Glue, see page 7
Gumpaste Glue, see page 7

EQUIPMENT

33cm (13 in) round cake board
no. 33 large plain single scallop crimper
nos. 2 and 1 piping tubes (tips)
parchment triangles ● boat mould
confectioners' glaze ● wooden satay sticks
polystyrene blocks ● cocktail sticks (toothpicks)
non-stick teflon-coated cloth
metal meat skewer

● Cover the board with blue sugarpaste, taking it right down over the edge and cut a scalloped edge with the crimper. Marble the remaining blue sugarpaste with white and coat the cake. Work it into the ridges of marzipan pinching the waves as for the marzipan, see page 40.

● Leave to dry. Brush the waves with white royal icing. Pipe the decoration of waves around the base of the cake using a royal icing and a no. 2 plain piping tube (tip).

● If you make a mould, use the outlines shown. When it is complete, sand away the section shown by the dotted line, see diagram page 40.

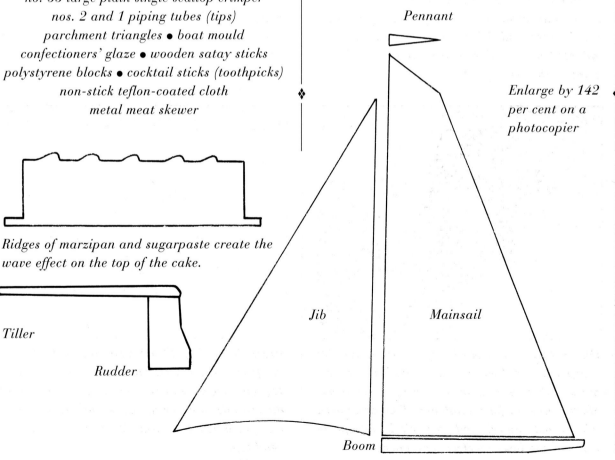

Ridges of marzipan and sugarpaste create the wave effect on the top of the cake.

Tiller

Rudder

Pennant

Jib

Mainsail

Boom

Enlarge by 142 per cent on a photocopier

ASSEMBLING THE DINGHY

Fit the mast into the hull. To do this, burn a hole through the hull and the icing underneath with a hot metal skewer. Then push a wooden satay stick through the hole into the cake, at the same angle of heel as the boat hull. Remove it and insert the royal icing mast. Mark the position for the bottom of the sail, pipe a line of royal icing down the leading edge of the mainsail and stick it to the mast, supporting it with pieces of foam sponge; leave to dry.

The leading edge of the jib is the longest side of the triangle. Stick the pointed ends to the hull and the mast with gumpaste glue and support it with foam or polystyrene until it sets. Finally, connect the right-angled corner of the jib to the hull with rope made from a thin strip of hardened pastillage. Although it may look fragile, the jib is then firmly secured to the boat at three points, and it is actually quite strong.

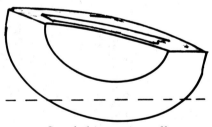

Sand this section off

EXPERT ADVICE
≈

Pastillage dries quickly on balsa wood because its surface is slightly rough and it contains millions of tiny air pockets. Plastic moulds are very smooth, impervious to air, and consequently result in slower drying.

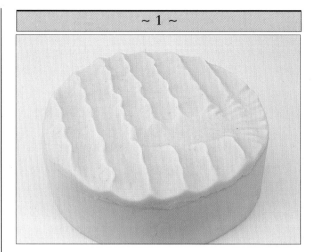

~ 1 ~

Marzipan the cake, then roll seven 1cm (½ in) diameter marzipan cylinders and stick them across the cake top. Smooth them and pinch them to form the wave tops. Use the boat mould to squash part of the middle four rows. Leave to harden for at least 24 hours.

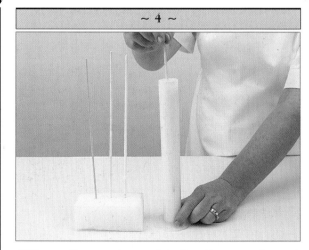

~ 4 ~

Fill a tall container with flooding consistency royal icing. Dip a satay stick into the icing, remove and set it in a polystyrene block to allow the excess to run off. When dry, dip again and repeat until the icing completely conceals the stick. This is the mast.

~ 2 ~

Carve a hull mould in a block of balsa wood which is easy to shape using a craft knife and medium grade sandpaper. Shape the pastillage hull over the upturned mould. Leave to harden.

~ 3 ~

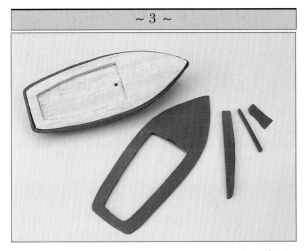

Make the decking on the upper side of the mould. Dry, then join to the hull with gumpaste glue. Make the boom, rudder and tiller from brown pastillage. Varnish with two or three coats of confectioners' glaze. Stick onto the cake with royal icing.

~ 5 ~

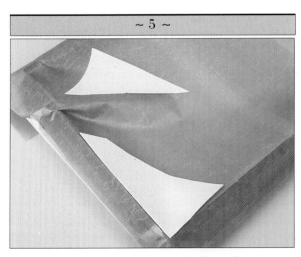

Stretch a non-stick mat or polythene bag over a square cake tin and tape it taut. Place a heavy object in the centre to make it sag. Cut out thin white pastillage sails. Rest them on the mat so that as they dry, the body of each sail curves while the edges remain straight.

~ 6 ~

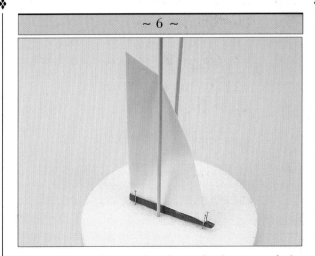

When the sails are hard, stick the top of the boom to the shortest edge of the mainsail with royal icing or gumpaste glue and support it between a pair of satay sticks until it has dried.

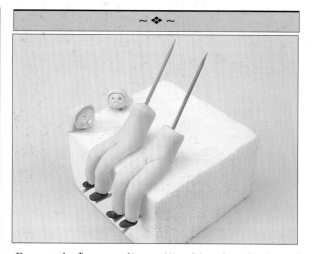

For each figure: slit a 15g (½ oz) cylinder of yellow paste almost halfway lengthways. Roll and bend the slit sections into legs. Secure on a polystyrene block with cocktail sticks (toothpicks). Attach feet and support with cocktail sticks until dry. Make the heads with yellow sowesters; dry, then attach with royal icing.

Fix the crew to boat with gumpaste glue. When set, add the rudder, tiller, arms and hands holding the tiller and ropes. Make scarves to conceal the neck joints, supporting until set. Roll very thin strands of pastillage for ropes and attach as shown.

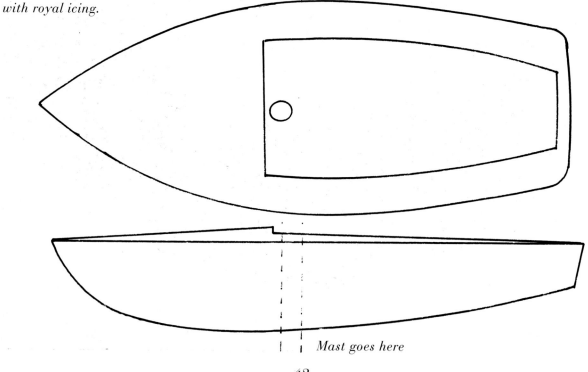

Mast goes here

DUCK AND FOX

*T*he languid reclining fox has an air of confidence and menace as he observes Mrs Duck trotting innocently along the country path. The unofficial title for this cake is 'Lunch'.

30 x 25cm (12 x 10 in) scalloped oval cake
1.25kg (2½ lb) marzipan (almond paste)
1.5kg (3 lb) sugarpaste ● apricot glaze
selection of paste and dusting powder (petal dust/blossom tint) food colourings
Gum Arabic Glue, see page 7
piping ge ● gum tragacanth
small amount of royal icing
250g (8 oz) Pastillage (2) or (3), see page 6
Gumpaste Glue, see page 7

EQUIPMENT

35 x 30cm (14 x 12 in) scalloped oval cake board
nos. 0, 32R ribbon and 50, 51 and 52 leaf piping tubes (tips)
non-stick teflon-coated cloth
parchment triangles ● confectioners' glaze
modelling tools ● 20swg coated wire
set of teardrop-shaped cutters
wooden cocktail sticks (toothpicks)
polystyrene blocks

Remove a saucer-shaped piece approximately 20 cm (8 in) across from the middle of the cake, see diagram below. Coat the cake with marzipan. Make a sausage from the leftover marzipan and drape it over the cake following the dotted line in the diagram. Smooth it into the surface to form the shape for the footpath. Place the cake to the back of the cake board. Use small pieces of marzipan to build up an area to support the fox. Allow the marzipan to harden for 24 hours before covering the cake and board with green sugarpaste.

● While the coating is still soft, make the surface of the footpath by rolling out a piece of beige-coloured sugarpaste about 30cm (12 in) long and 10cm (4 in) wide at one end, tapering

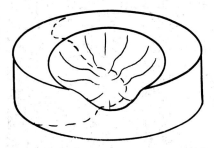

Cut a saucer-shaped piece out of the cake, then marzipan it

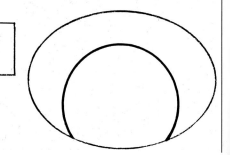

Cross-section through centre of cake

to about 2.5cm (1 in) at the other end. Paint the surface of the cake where the path is to be positioned with gum arabic glue and lay the beige strip over it, with the wide end resting on the cake board at the front. Smooth the strip into the green sugarpaste, then texture it to look like a sandy path and dust with brown and cream dusting powders.

● Make the stone foundation for the wide end of the path by pressing sugar pebbles, see page 18, into the soft sugarpaste, extending down the side of the cake from its top to the board. Stick each pebble with gum arabic glue and arrange small weeds and grass in the crevices. Make bushes and shrubs using the techniques on pages 18 and 19 and arrange on the cake.

● Boil the piping gel and spoon it into place beside the path while it is still warm; then arrange more grass at the water's edge.

MARZIPAN MODELLING

Most of the models in this book have been made with pastillage, but modelling with marzipan is also great fun. Prepare the marzipan at least 12 hours before use: knead 5ml (1 tsp) gum tragacanth into 250g (8 oz) white marzipan (almond paste). If the paste appears dry or crumbly, add 5ml (1 tsp) liquid glucose (clear corn syrup) and add a little more icing (confectioners') sugar if a whiter paste is required. Knead the paste well to bring out the almond oils.

MR FOX When working on complex models, like the fox, that take several days to complete, place the pieces in a plastic bag or airtight plastic container for a few hours before continuing to allow them to set but not crust. If they get too hard, steam them for a few seconds

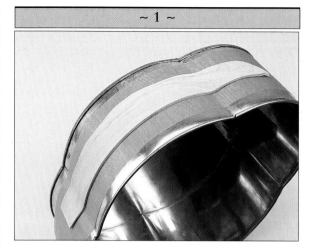

~ 1 ~

WALL The low stone wall on the cake is made on a pastillage foundation. Tape a piece of non-stick cloth to the side of the tin in which the cake was baked. Cut a strip of light brown pastillage following the template on page 66. Rest this on the side of the tin to harden.

~ 1 ~

FOX Shape 30g (1 oz) marzipan and pierce with a cocktail stick. Shape the snout. Cut the jaws and widen the top from inside using a veining tool. Model the upper jaw and nose. Smooth a pea-sized piece of white marzipan under the chin. Leave under plastic wrap for 12 hours.

~ 2 ~

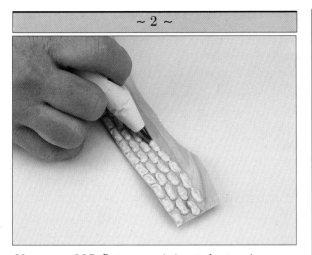

Use a no. 32R flat rope piping tube to pipe rows of stones about 2cm (¾ in) long onto the hardened pastillage. Do not make the pattern too regular. Profile some of the stones by drawing a damp paintbrush through the freshly piped royal icing.

~ 3 ~

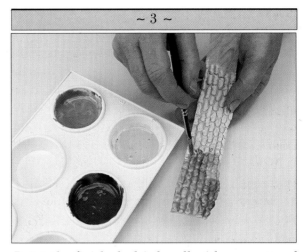

Paint the finished, dried wall with runny royal icing coloured dark green, brown and cream to make the wall appear dry in some places and damp in others. Roll a cylinder of paste to the height of the wall for the fence post. Scratch the surface, then paint it to match the wall.

~ 2 ~

Pinch the head top; shape the eye sockets with a dogbone tool and insert a teardrop piece of white marzipan in each. Smooth two small, tapered cylinders of chestnut paste into place for eyelids. Use a modelling stick to wrinkle the snout, from nose to eyes. Add a pink tongue.

~ 3 ~

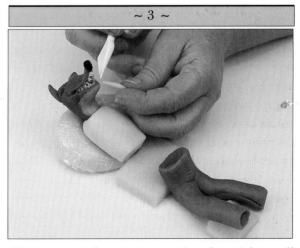

The ears are brown paste triangles with small triangles of white paste inside. Add a nose of black paste: mark the centre line and dots for nostrils. Add the teeth, back to front, from a thin roll of paste. to the front. Hollow the body cylinder top and fix the head in place.

in the vapour from a boiling kettle. This will also revive the colours. When colouring marzipan remember that it is not white, so the final colours will not be as pure as when using pastillage. You will need about 90 – 125g (3 – 4 oz) marzipan: 30g (1 oz) for the head, 45g (1½ oz) for the body and 15g (½ oz) for the arms and legs.

● Always start by making the head, as this will establish the scale of the figure. Before modelling the head, prepare a simple support for it by pressing your thumb into a pad of marzipan to make a hollow which will hold the head while you work on the details. Cover with plastic wrap. Follow the steps for modelling the head. The body is a cylinder of white paste, hollowed at the neck end, and the legs are made from a cylinder about the same length as the head and torso. Cut the legs as for the sailor's legs, see page 42, then roll and shape them as in the final step.

DUCK The steps, opposite, show the stages in making the duck. Roll 45g (1½ oz) of pastillage it into a pear shape, then bend it into the outline of the diagram, see right. Insert two curved pieces of 20swg covered wire 1cm (½ in) apart into the base, so that they project from the thin end of paste where they will eventually meet to support the head. Make the webbed feet from two pea-sized cones of paste. Flatten and mark them with a modelling knife. Make a hole through the back of each foot with a 20swg wire, then leave the feet to harden. To make feathers which will cover the body of the duck, use a selection of small teardrop-shaped cutters to cut the pastillage. Use a fine palette knife or a craft knife, to cut the wider end of each piece of paste into fine strands or 'feathers'. When the body is complete and dry, cut out a jacket of

thinly rolled pastillage to encase the body, then work it by hand to form the head over the projecting wires. Finally, make a shawl from a triangle of mauve pastillage, and crimp and frill the bottom edge. Attach the bows of the bonnet before adding the crown and brim. Decorate the brim by cutting tiny holes with a no. 0 piping tube. Carefully dress the duck and leave to dry.

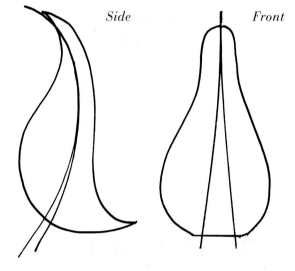

Side   *Front*

This is the basic duck shape, showing how the reinforcing wires are used

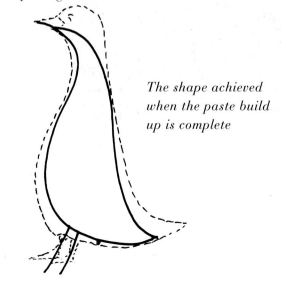

The shape achieved when the paste build up is complete

~ 1 ~

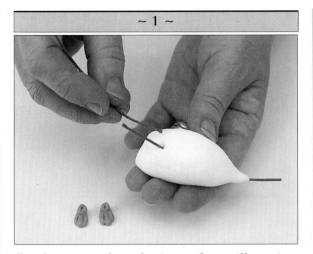

Bend a pear-shaped piece of pastillage into shape, then insert the wires which hold the feet and eventually meet at the thin end to support the head. Push them in from the broad end of the paste.

~ 2 ~

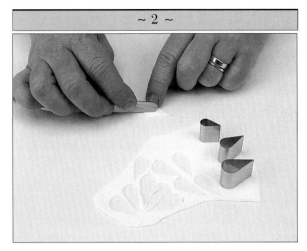

Make sufficient feathers to cover the duck. Use teardrop cutters to make them different sizes. Cut the wide end of each into fine strands and stick them in place before they have time to harden.

~ 3 ~

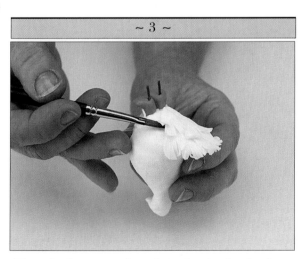

Glue the feet onto the wires. Apply the feathers, overlapping, from tail to feet, then up the body. The feathers become smaller towards the head. Use a soft brush to lift the feather tips.

~ 4 ~

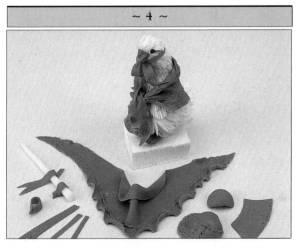

Paint the beak bright orange and mark the eyes. Make the clothes and fit them carefully onto the duck. Use frilling techniques to create folds and creases in the garments.

TUDOR COTTAGE

*T*his cottage has been set in a winter scene by coating the square cake board with white sugarpaste, and sprinkling it with sugartex 'snow'. The black timber beams and bowed tiled roof help to give this little cottage an air of permanence and antiquity. In practice the opposite is true. I put the roof on too soon, when the paste wasn't completely hard, so it sagged more than I had intended!

1kg (2 lb) Pastillage (1), see page 6
selection of paste and dusting powder (petal dust/blossom tint) food colourings
250g (8 oz) sugarpaste
small amount of royal icing ● white sugartex
Gum Arabic Glue, see page 7
Gumpaste Glue, see page 7
2 sheets leaf gelatine
EQUIPMENT
23cm (9 in) square cake board
no. 1.5 piping tube (tip) ● parchment triangles
confectioners' glaze ● polystyrene blocks
4cm (1½ in) crimper
or straight Garrett frill cutter

● Colour 185g (6 oz) of the pastillage with red and chestnut brown for the tiles, 90g (3 oz) black and 90g (3 oz) dark brown.

● Cut the walls from white paste and allow them to harden for 24 hours. Be very careful to ensure that they are scaled to be in precisely the same proportion as your templates. When you have cut them out, lay the templates on top and check the wall pieces for accuracy.

● Cut the window frames and doors from the dark brown paste and the roof panels, see page 67, from the reddish-brown paste. Leave to dry at least 24 hours, turning the pieces over occasionally so that they do not warp.

● Assemble the cottage, then conceal the joints behind extra strips of black pastillage half-timbering. Add the chimney and the loading beam with its hook, and pipe the hinges and knocker onto the cottage door.

● Transfer the cottage to its cake board, and set it in position with royal icing. Add the final embellishments – use small lumps of sugarpaste to make hummocks of drifting snow, and pipe white royal icing along the edge of the tiles. While the icing is still wet, place the cottage on a large tray and sprinkle it with white sugartex or a mixture of sugartex and icing sugar if you prefer a softer dusting of snowflakes.

EXPERT ADVICE

≈

Secure the gelatine with a dot of royal icing at each corner of the window frame. Do not attempt to seal it all around the frame as the gelatine is very unstable, and any change in humidity will cause it to flex and warp. If it is completely stuck down, it will buckle and damage the paste around the window.

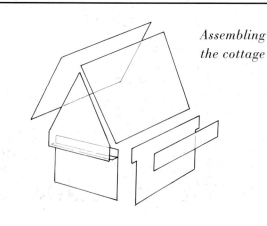

Assembling the cottage

Enlarge by 200 per cent on a photocopier

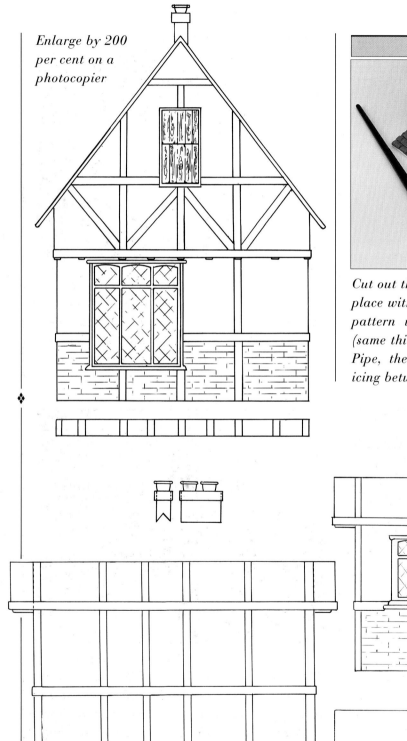

Cut out the side pieces in red pastillage: glue in place with gum arabic glue; indent a brickwork pattern while soft. Make the window frame (same thickness as brickwork). Attach the door. Pipe, then brush cream or light brown royal icing between brickwork.

~ 2 ~

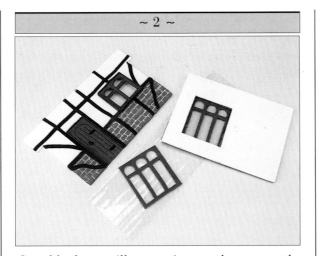

Cut black pastillage strips to lay over the brickwork and upper walls; attach with gum arabic glue while soft. Attach outer window frames using brown royal icing or gumpaste glue; set. Cut leaf gelatine panes and apply to frames from the inside.

~ 3 ~

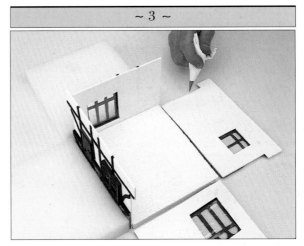

Cut a rectangular pad of board or polystyrene to the same size as the length and breadth of the house. Assemble one side and one end, using the rectangular pad as a guide so that the corner of the house is joined at a right angle.

~ 4 ~

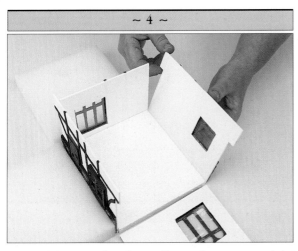

Join the second side wall to the two upright pieces, supporting each of the pieces until set. Reinforce the upper corners of the building with small polystyrene blocks, stuck in place with royal icing. Add both upper end sections and support with polystyrene until set.

~ 5 ~

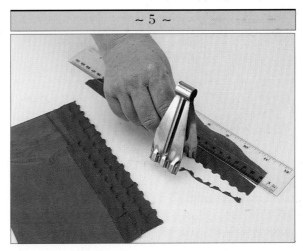

Cut strips of tiles from thin paste using the 4cm (1½ in) crimper or Garrett frill cutter. Stick each strip as it is made, from the roof bottom upwards, overlapping each strip. Dry for least 24 hours. Fix one side firmly before attaching the second.

FAIRIES

*A*n entrancing open-air performance of *A Midsummer Night's Dream* provided the inspiration for this cake-top decoration. Titania, the Queen of the fairies, and Puck are shown planning some mischief while they unravel a long band of silken ribbon. The figures, mushrooms and ribbon are all pastillage and the decorative frieze is traced, see page 68, and painted directly onto the icing with food colouring and a fine sable brush.

20cm (8 in) hexagonal cake
625g (1¼ lb) marzipan (almond paste)
1.5kg (3 lb) sugarpaste
apricot glaze
selection of paste and dusting powder (petal dust/blossom tint) food colourings
250g (8 oz) Pastillage (2) or (3), see page 6
highlighting lustre colourings: peach, russet and mother-of-pearl
small amount of royal icing
Gumpaste Glue, see page 7
Gum Arabic Glue, see page 7
E Q U I P M E N T
30cm (12 in) hexagonal thin cake board
no. 14 mini double scallop crimper
1.5m (1⅔ yd) x 3mm (⅛ in) peach ribbon
small people torso moulds ● daisy-leaf cutter
bramble leaf silicone veiner
polystyrene blocks
wooden cocktail sticks (toothpicks)
star cutter
nos. 0 and 1 piping tubes (tips)
parchment triangles ● wooden frame
confectioners' glaze ● tracing wheel
Garrett frill cutter ● large-headed pins
20swg coated wire

● Marzipan the cake and cover with peach-coloured sugarpaste. Set the cake on a hexagonal board which has been covered with peach sugarpaste. Crimp the sugarpaste edge and trim the edge of the board with the ribbon.

● Make the fairies in sections, forming the torsos in plastic moulds and shaping the arms and legs freehand, see page 57. When the bodies and legs are dry, dress the figures.

● For Titania, use the daisy-leaf cutter and cut out about six pieces of very pale peach paste. Vein each one with the veiner and then dust with peach or mother of pearl highlighter. Keep the other pieces covered while you work so that they do not dry out. Drape the tips of five or six leaves around the waist of the figure, arranging the leaves so that they follow the curve of the legs. Stick the figure with gumpaste glue or royal icing to the top of one of the mushrooms. Attach the arms and leave the model to set, supported on polystyrene or foam sponge.

● When the arms are set, dress the upper body and attach the wings. Cut another four daisy leaves, two for the front and two for the back, veining and dusting them as before and attach them at the shoulders, letting them drape around the arms and body.

● Make the hair from very thinly rolled bright orange pastillage, cut into narrow strands with a fine palette knife. Wind them around a cocktail stick (toothpick) to form ringlets and leave them to dry partially for a few minutes. Stick them to the head with gum arabic glue, working from the neck up to the crown of the head, making sure that the top of each strand is covered by the ringlet above it. Make a coronet using a star cutter and punch tiny holes into the points with the tip of a no. 0 piping tube (tip).

● When the wings are dry and painted, attach

them with gumpaste glue and support until set.

○ Use richly coloured chestnut pastillage to make the man's lower half. Leave to dry suspended in a wooden frame, see page 57. While still suspended from the frame, dress his upper body by cutting out a small piece of bright orange paste using the template shown on page 58 as a guide. Stick the shirt front to his chest and turn the collar section back. Make orange coloured sleeves, pleating the paste at the wrists and the top of the arms. Use orange gumpaste glue or royal icing to attach the arms, then support them with polystyrene while they set.

○ Cut the back of his jerkin from thinly rolled light brown paste and attach it neatly. Paint a line of gum arabic glue across the shoulders and down the side seam. Cut two squares of paste for the front, gather the top and bottom edge and drape them from the shoulders, gathering them at the waist. Trim the surplus with scissors. For the bottom half of the jerkin, gather a rectangle of paste slightly at the top and attach around the waist. Leave it open at the front, and drape it over the raised knee. Make a gumpaste belt and small pouch and glue them into place.

○ Make the hair from finely fringed strips of white pastillage and attach them by winding them around the head, working from the forehead and neck up to the crown. Paint the surface of the toadstool with a russet-coloured highlighter mixed with confectioners' glaze and stick it on the cake, then position the fairy. When he is secure, attach his wings.

○ To make the ribbon, roll out and flatten a long sausage of paste and cut a narrow strip using a ruler and palette knife. Run a tracing wheel along each edge to look like its binding. Remember to keep one end covered while you work the other end.

~ 1 ~

To make the mushrooms, marble a 60g (2 oz) ball of paste with dark brown food colouring. Divide it into three, the largest piece of about 45g (1½ oz) for the cap. Shape it into a dome with a slightly indented base. Cut fine lines on the base radiating out from the centre to the edge of the cap and leave to dry. Divide the remaining paste in half: roll one piece into a cone and dry on a cocktail stick (toothpick); roll out the other piece and cut a circle with a Garrett frill cutter. Frill it around the edge and glue it to the surface of the cap. When the stalk is hard, glue the top to it with royal icing.

~ 2 ~

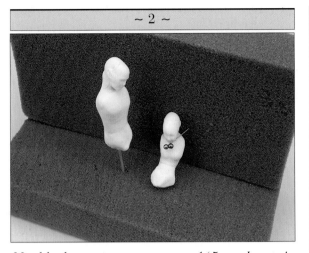

Mould the torsos, see page 145 and set in position to dry – the man with his head looking down, while lady's body is twisted into a sitting position and supported against a piece of polystyrene by large pins crossed under the chin.

~ 3 ~

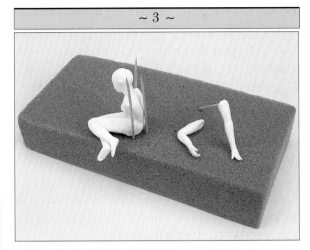

When the lady's body is dry, mould the legs, see page 13. Stick them to the torso with gumpaste glue, bending them and hanging the feet over the edge of the mushroom on which she is to sit. Support until dry. Make the arms and hands freehand and bend to the desired shape.

~ 4 ~

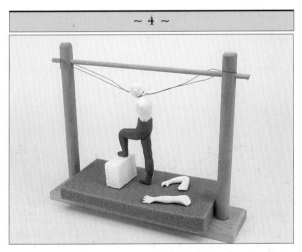

Make the man's straight leg first, insert wire into the foot and ankle and attach with gumpaste glue; hang from the neck to dry. Make the second leg, bending it at the knee, and support until hardened. Shape the arms and hands and leave to dry.

~ 5 ~

Cut the wings from finely rolled pastillage. Paint with dusting colourings and highlighters. Frill the lady's wing edges and fold the man's. When the wings are dried, attach to dressed figures and place on the cake.

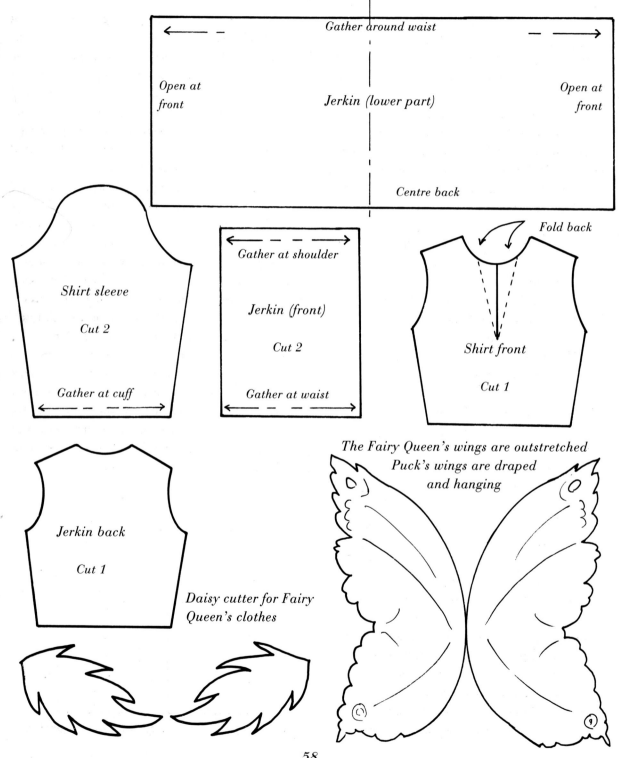

Gather around waist

Open at front

Jerkin (lower part)

Open at front

Centre back

Shirt sleeve

Cut 2

Gather at cuff

Gather at shoulder

Jerkin (front)

Cut 2

Gather at waist

Fold back

Shirt front

Cut 1

Jerkin back

Cut 1

Daisy cutter for Fairy Queen's clothes

The Fairy Queen's wings are outstretched
Puck's wings are draped
and hanging

TABLEAU

*E*very part of the furnishings and the figures in this tableau of a Victorian melodrama was made from sugar and the scene illustrates the value of using more than one recipe for pastillage. One mixture was chosen because of its suitability for building walls and the chimney breast, while the other was softer and ideal for draping into the folds and creases of the curtains and for clothing the figures.

500g (1 lb) sugarpaste
selection of paste and dusting powder
(petal dust/blossom tint) food colourings
small amount of royal icing
1kg (2 lb) Pastillage (1), see page 6, for walls and chimney
1.5kg (3 lb) Pastillage (3), see page 6, for figures, clothes and curtains
Gum Arabic Glue, see page 7
Gumpaste Glue, see page 7
red and black jelly sweets
EQUIPMENT
46cm (18 in) round thick cake board
1cm (½ in) square wooden beading
superglue
33cm (13 in) square and 33 x 25cm
(13 x 10 in) thin cake boards
stiff bristle brush or foam sponge
polystyrene and foam sponge blocks
small metal hinge ● large daisy cutters
confectioners' glaze ● gold and silver paint
large people moulds ● wooden satay sticks
modelling stick ● ribbed rolling pin
wooden cocktail sticks (toothpicks)
nos. 42, 0 and 1 piping tubes (tips)
parchment triangles ● dog mould
no. 33 large single scallop crimper

● Prepare the base by gluing two strips of wooden beading to the surface of a 45cm (18 in) round cake board – these act as supports for the base of the walls, and should be positioned at between 90 and 100 degrees to one another, with their ends just meeting. A rapid drying liquid superglue is satisfactory for this purpose.

● Cover the 33cm (13 in) square cake board with brown sugarpaste. Cut off a 5cm (2 in) wide strip of the brown paste from one edge, and replace it with a strip of white paste. Dry.

● Make the panels for the chimney breast and the fireplace, the mantelpiece, the pieces for the mirror and the framework for the wall panelling using the templates on page 67. Dry. Use royal icing to secure them, beginning with the curved fireplace back, then the sides of the chimney breast, the front and, finally, the fireplace.

● Overpipe the mirror frame and when dry, gild it and silver the mirror. Stipple a pattern onto the wallpapered area of the chimney: use a dry stiff brush or a piece of foam sponge to dab the colour onto the surface. Set the mantelpiece and marble front of the fireplace into position, glue

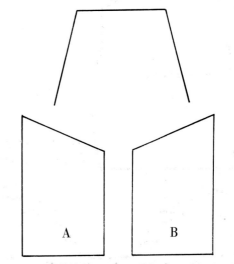

See Expert Advice, page 20, for perspective

the mirror in place and assemble the woodwork of the panelling. Add a narrow strip of pastillage for the picture rail but not the wider strip for the skirting board.

⬤ Cover the floor of the room with ivory-coloured sugarpaste, leaving a 5mm (¼ in) gap between the paste and the timber beading. Texture the paste for carpet, see page 19.

⬤ Make up a quantity of navy blue pastillage for the curtains. Roll it out very thinly and lay it in folds over the rectangular thin cake board, sticking it down firmly at the top edge. Roll out a strip of paste about 45 x 15cm (18 x 6 in) and gather this into swags along the curtain tops.

⬤ Glue the chimney-wall board snugly into the slot between the carpet and beading on the base board, to stand upright against the wooden beading. Prop up the panel. Then apply superglue to the curtained board and place it in its slot against the other length of beading. Be careful not to damage the folds in the draped curtain. Glue a small metal hinge across the joint close to the top of the panels to hold them together. Hold the hinge until the glue dries. Arrange the drapes and folds of the curtains to conceal the join between panels. Finally, stick the skirting board along the bottom of the wall.

⬤ Make the grate from black pastillage by cutting out two daisy shapes, then overlay them on top of each over a small domed dish. Attach four small round feet and leave to dry. Paint with confectioners' glaze. Cut up red and black jelly sweets and place in the grate to represent coals. Mould a small piece of paste into the clock shape, then pipe on the decoration using royal icing and dry before gilding. Stick in position on the mantelpiece with royal icing.

Templates for clothing on pages 69 – 71

THE GENTLEMAN

⬤ Mould the gentleman's torso and legs using a two-part mould as shown on page 14. Incline the head so that it is looking up and position the legs so that he is kneeling on one knee. Make a cut at the back of the knee and at the buttocks so that the leg bends easily. Push a wooden satay stick right down the leg and out through the knee to reinforce the paste to support the weight of the figure.

⬤ Complete the head. Assemble the legs and torso, then follow the steps, right, for applying the physical features.

⬤ Dress the man: start with the boots by wrapping a very thin strip of black paste around each foot. Cut a sole for each boot and attach it with gum arabic glue. Trim around the edges with nail scissors and mark the heel and bootlaces with a modelling tool. Cut one trouser leg at a time, letting the paste crease naturally at the groin and around the knees. Cut off any excess paste with the nail scissors as you fit the trousers to the figure.

⬤ Use a ribbed rolling pin to pleat the shirt front and fix it on the figure. Attach a wing collar to the shirt, then roll out a narrow strip for the neck tie. Make a cravat and glue it into folds down the shirt front before attaching the waistcoat. Cut each side of the topcoat and attach with gum arabic glue, joining down the centre back to the waist, letting the paste crease naturally into folds.

⬤ Make the arms and hands and attach the shirt cuffs before making the sleeves of the coat from black paste. Colour some gumpaste glue black, attach the arms with it and support them with pieces of foam sponge and polystyrene blocks until they have set in place. Use the remaining

~ 1 ~

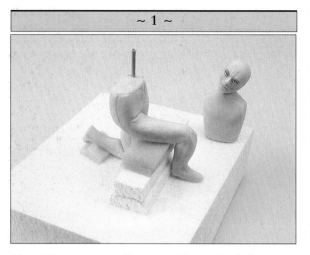

THE GENTLEMAN Support the raised knee on polystyrene and foam sponge until it has set in this position. When the torso is dry, paint the eyes, see page 12.

~ 2 ~

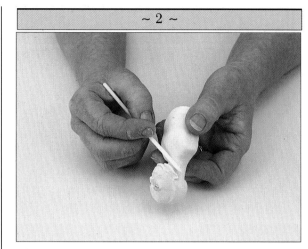

As this gentleman has a mature, portly figure, he has been given a double chin. Roll two very small cylinders of skin coloured paste and use a modelling stick to smooth them into place under the chin. Add the ears, see page 12.

~ 5 ~

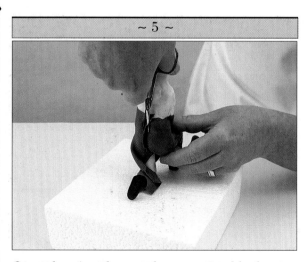

Start dressing the man by wrapping black paste on his feet, for boots. Then apply the trousers, cutting the paste to fit, and ease them onto the shape of the figure. Allow the paste to fold and crease around the knee and buttocks.

~ 6 ~

Cut out and rib the shirt, then glue it in place. Add the wing collar, neck tie and cravat. Make the waistcoat and attach both sides to the model. Note the floral pattern, made by rolling tiny cut-out pastillage flowers into the waistcoat paste.

~ 3 ~

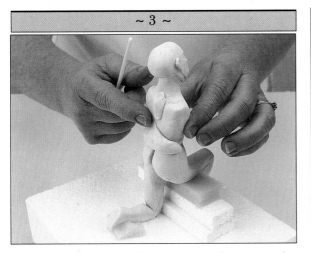

Stick the torso to the legs and leave to dry before attaching a roll of paste to the waistline at the back and another to the area between the shoulder blades. This padding will add definition to the body when concealed under the jacket.

~ 4 ~

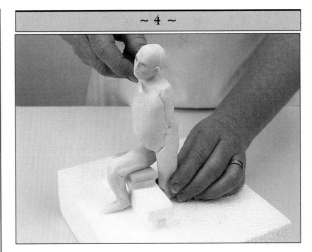

Roll a piece of skin-coloured paste into a flattened egg shape and glue this to the front of the figure to enlarge the chest and belly. Smooth all the join lines with a modelling stick. When the figure has dried out completely, the model can be dressed.

~ 7 ~

When the figure is dressed and the arms are fixed, the details of the hair and whiskers are painted on using black-coloured gumpaste glue, applied with a very fine sable brush.

~ 8 ~

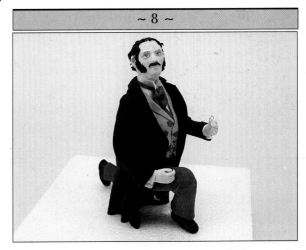

The completed figure shows in detail the way in which the pastillage jacket and trousers have been arranged so that they have natural-looking folds and creases.

black gumpaste glue to paint the side whiskers, receding hairline and bald patch. Make a tiny engagement ring by rolling a very small sausage of paste around a cocktail stick. When dry, gild it and put it into the raised hand.

When the figure is complete, it can be moved to the tableau scene. Make a hole in the carpet to accommodate the satay stick which protrudes from the knee.

THE LADY

Only the torso need be moulded, for as this lady has a long skirt she will be more stable with a pillar to support her rather than a pair of legs. Make a small cone of green paste to represent the front part of a shoe and attach this to the base of the pillar. Roll out a strip of white paste and drape this around the base of the pillar, lifting it slightly so that the shoe protrudes from beneath it.

Roll out a rectangle of dark green paste for the skirt and stick this around the pillar. Attach a dome-shape piece of paste at the back for a bustle. Roll out a rectangle of green paste and attach as a drape to the front, flattening all the pleats and cutting away any excess paste. Frill a collar and wrap it around the neck. The hem of the skirt is decorated with a ribbed piece of light green paste and rosettes of light and dark paste.

Add the light green waistcoat next. Place a piece of light green paste which has rib-rolled pleats inside the jacket edge so that it will show when the lapels are turned back. Add the collar and the frilled jabot before fixing the jacket to the figure. Use a no. 0 piping tube (tip) to pipe a scalloped line around the edge of the jacket and the buttons.

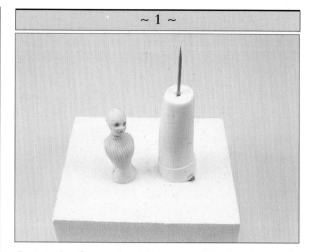

~ 1 ~

Paint the face, then using a ribbed rolling pin to create pleats, roll a piece of cream paste for the front of the blouse and attach to the torso. The pillar is used to support the torso instead of legs.

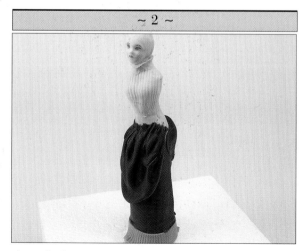

~ 2 ~

Attach the torso to the pillar. Stick on the basic skirt, then add the drape at the front and the bustle at the back. Place ribbed green paste and rosette trimming around the base.

● Model the arms and hands, cover them with sleeves before leaving to set in place. Cut a pair of gloves out of thinly rolled light green paste and place them in the right hand. Make sure that the train falls into elegant folds before covering the bustle and the top of the train with another drape. Use a no. 1 piping tube (tip) and brown royal icing to pipe the hair into ringlets. Mould a tricorn hat and decorate it with feathers and bows.

Position for
1 *dog,*
2 *kneeling man,*
3 *lady*

TEMPLATES

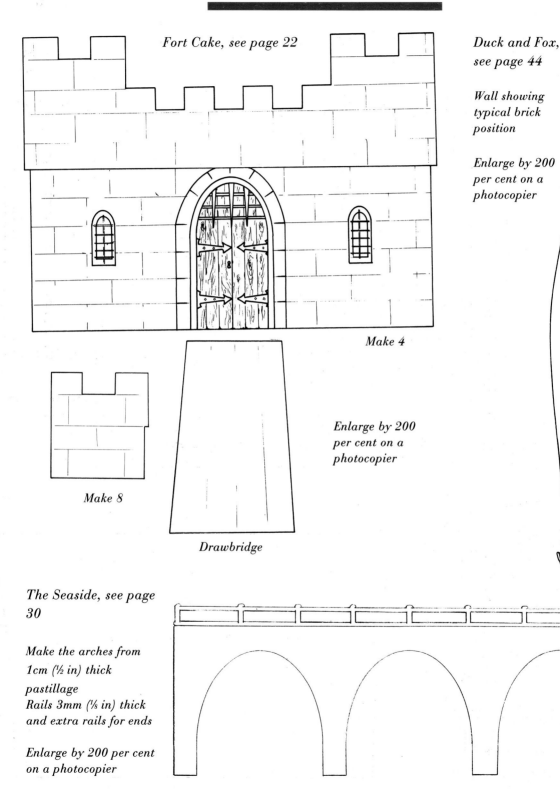

Fort Cake, see page 22

Make 4

Make 8

Enlarge by 200 per cent on a photocopier

Drawbridge

Duck and Fox, see page 44

Wall showing typical brick position

Enlarge by 200 per cent on a photocopier

The Seaside, see page 30

Make the arches from 1cm (½ in) thick pastillage
Rails 3mm (⅛ in) thick and extra rails for ends

Enlarge by 200 per cent on a photocopier

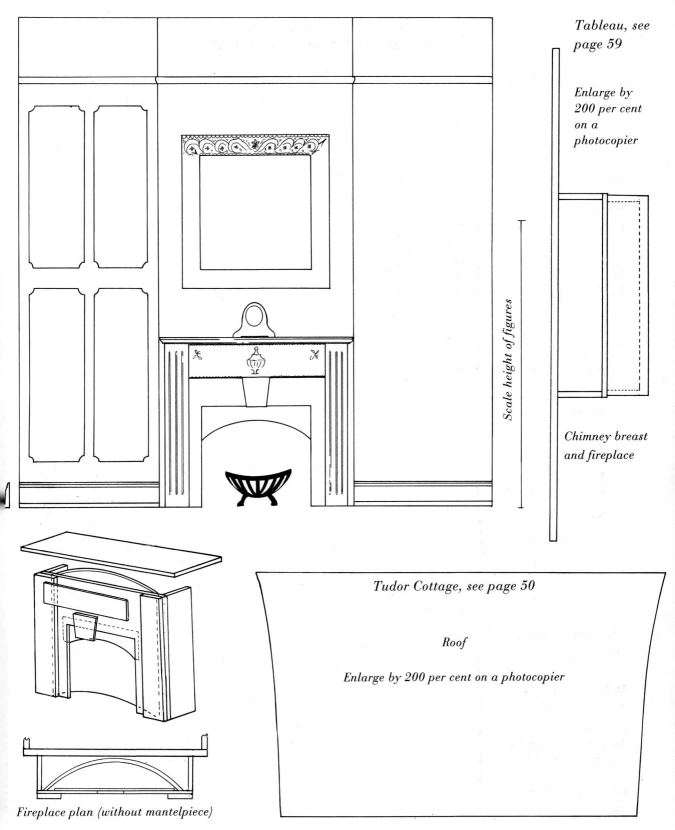

Tableau, see page 59

Enlarge by 200 per cent on a photocopier

Scale height of figures

Chimney breast and fireplace

Tudor Cottage, see page 50

Roof

Enlarge by 200 per cent on a photocopier

Fireplace plan (without mantelpiece)

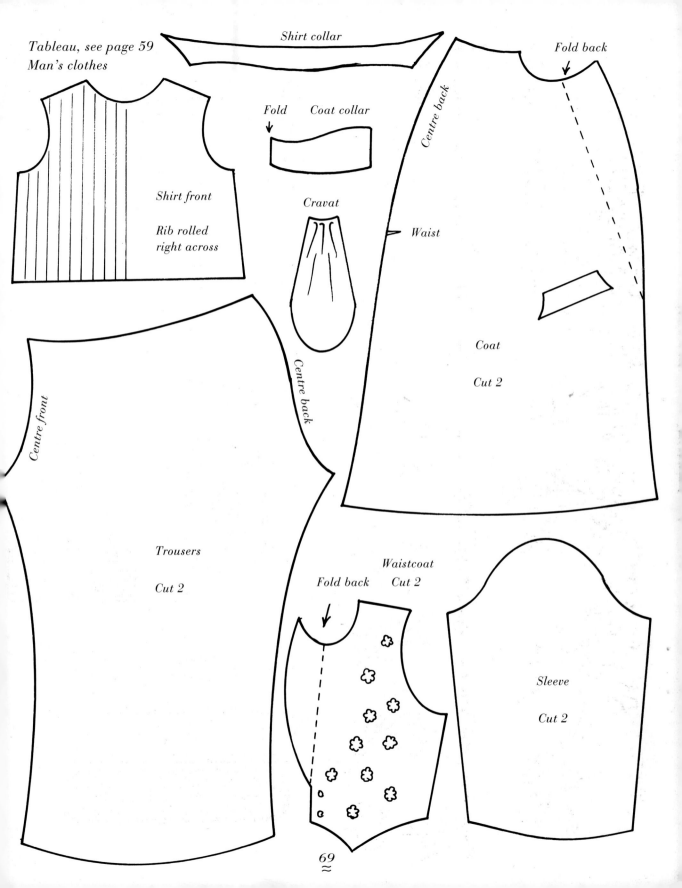

Tableau, see page 59
Man's clothes

Shirt collar

Fold   Coat collar

Shirt front

Rib rolled
right across

Cravat

Centre back

Fold back

Centre back

Waist

Coat

Cut 2

Centre front

Trousers

Cut 2

Waistcoat
Cut 2

Fold back

Sleeve

Cut 2

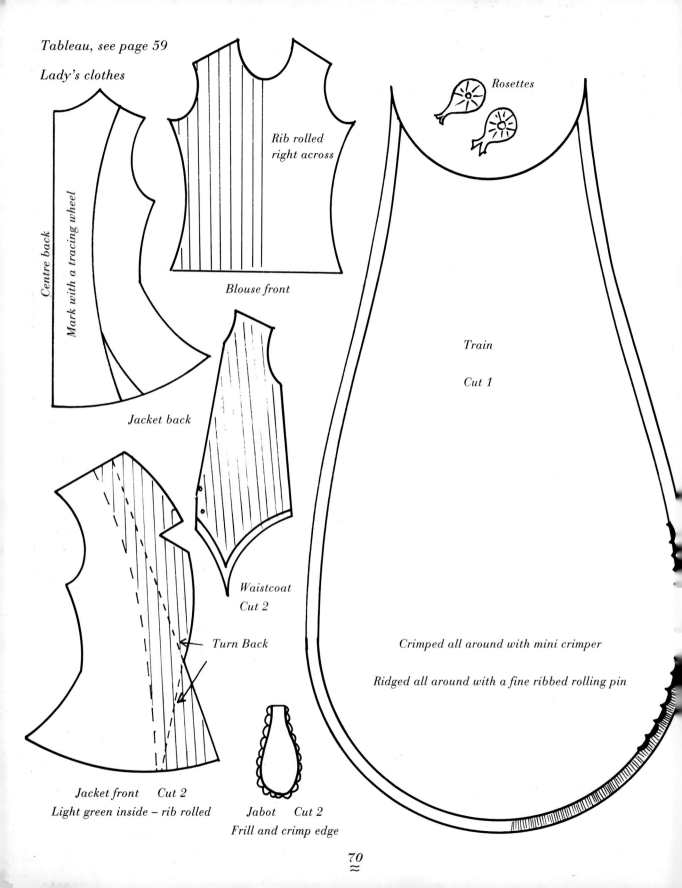

Tableau, see page 59

Lady's clothes

Centre back

Mark with a tracing wheel

Rib rolled
right across

Blouse front

Rosettes

Jacket back

Train

Cut 1

Waistcoat
Cut 2

Turn Back

Crimped all around with mini crimper

Ridged all around with a fine ribbed rolling pin

Jacket front   Cut 2
Light green inside – rib rolled

Jabot   Cut 2
Frill and crimp edge

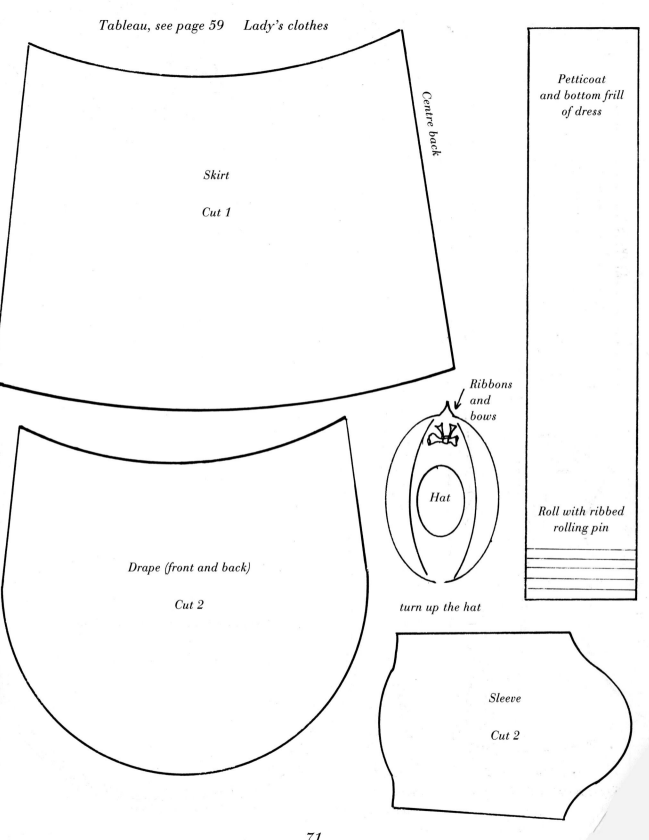

Tableau, see page 59   Lady's clothes

Skirt

Cut 1

Centre back

Petticoat
and bottom frill
of dress

Ribbons
and
bows

Hat

Drape (front and back)

Cut 2

turn up the hat

Roll with ribbed
rolling pin

Sleeve

Cut 2

INDEX

FOR FURTHER INFORMATION

Merehurst is the leading publisher of cake decorating books and has an excellent range of titles to suit cake decorators of all levels. Please send for a free catalogue, stating the title of this book:

United Kingdom
*Marketing Department
Merehurst Ltd.
Ferry House
51 -57 Lacy Road
...don SW15 1PR
...1 780 1177
...780 1714*

U.S.A./Canada
*Foxwood International Ltd.
P.O. Box 267
145 Queen Street S.
Missisauga, Ontario
L5M 2BS Canada
Tel: (1) 416 567 4800
Fax: (1) 416 567 4681*

Australia
*J.B. Fairfax Ltd.
80 McLachlan Avenue
Rushcutters Bay
NSW 2011
Tel: (61) 2 361 6366
Fax: (61) 2 360 6262*

Other Territories
*For further information
contact:
International Sales
Department at United
Kingdom address.*